Healing Richard Nixon

THE WHITE HOUSE

WASHINGTON

August 1, 1974

Dear Jack:

It is typical of you to always do the right
thing at the right time, and I deeply appreciate your thoughtful telegram of July 26.
Your words of friendship and concern mean
more than I can say, and they are a source
of strength and encouragement for me at
this difficult time.

Pat joins me in sending our warmest good
wishes to Lorain and you.

Sincerely,

Dr. John C. Lungren
4180 Chestnut Avenue
Long Beach, California

HEALING RICHARD NIXON

A DOCTOR'S MEMOIR

John C. Lungren, M.D.
and John C. Lungren Jr.

With a Foreword by Rick Perlstein

THE UNIVERSITY PRESS OF KENTUCKY

Publication of this volume was made possible in part by a grant from the National Endowment for the Humanities.

Scholarly publisher for the Commonwealth,
serving Bellarmine University, Berea College, Centre College of Kentucky, Eastern Kentucky University, The Filson Historical Society, Georgetown College, Kentucky Historical Society, Kentucky State University, Morehead State University, Murray State University, Northern Kentucky University, Transylvania University, University of Kentucky, University of Louisville, and Western Kentucky University.

Editorial and Sales Offices: The University Press of Kentucky
663 South Limestone Street, Lexington, Kentucky 40508-4008

07 06 05 04 03   5 4 3 2 1

Frontispiece: A letter to the author, sent by President Nixon just days before his resignation.

Library of Congress Cataloging-in-Publication Data
Lungren, John C., 1916-2000.
  Healing Richard Nixon : a doctor's memoir / John C. Lungren and John C. Lungren, Jr.
    p. cm.
  ISBN 0-8131-2274-0 (Cloth : alk. paper)
  1. Nixon, Richard M. (Richard Milhous), 1913—Health. 2. Nixon, Richard M. (Richard Milhous), 1913- 3. Presidents—United States—Biography. 4. Lungren, John C., 1916-2000. 5. Nixon, Richard M. (Richard Milhous), 1913—Friends and associates. 6. Physicians—United States—Biography. I. Lungren, John C. II. Title.
  E856.L86 2003
  973.924'092—dc21   2003005312

Manufactured in the United States of America.

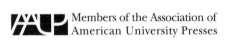

Members of the Association of American University Presses

Contents

Photos follow page 100

Foreword

Rick Perlstein

DR. JOHN C. LUNGREN BEGINS HIS BOOK with an epigraph from his subject. "But I have found that leaders are subject to all the human frailties," Richard Nixon wrote in his 1962 book *Six Crises*. It is a good choice, for the sentence suggests that Nixon once believed, remarkably, that somehow he could render himself invulnerable and that, well into his adulthood, he had to learn to live with the fact that he could not.

This quote also helps explain why Dr. John C. Lungren—not a biographer, not a historian, not a professional writer, certainly not an unbiased observer—is important for understanding Richard Nixon. This issue of vulnerability—repressing it, belatedly acknowledging it, fighting it, hiding it, probing it, exploiting it in others, and even, in strategic moments, exploiting it in himself—was central to Richard Nixon's life. As Richard Nixon's personal physician, John Lungren was on the campaign trails of the 1950s and 1960s, and he was with him after his resignation during the crisis of August 1974. Lungren was the one with the best access to Richard Nixon at those moments of existential crisis and physical vulnerability. It was Lungren who saw Nixon "alabaster white, incoherent, and slipping into unconsciousness" and who saw him being slapped back into consciousness by a nurse crying "Richard! Richard!"—the name no one but his dead mother had called him. Through him we see Nixon conveying information about his physical condition in humiliated whispers. There were no doubts at these moments about the great leader's equal vulnerability to human frailty. "Even the President of the United States," Bob Dylan sang, "sometimes must have to stand naked."

John C. Lungren was a California physician trained at the University of Notre Dame and the University of Pennsylvania, comfortably settled as a specialist in internal medicine and based at the Memorial Medical Center in Long Beach when he met Richard Nixon on his 1952 campaign train. He was soon asked to share duties as campaign physician. The two men were, in many ways, of a piece, which is to say, of a generation. They were men who had joined the effort to defeat Hitler and Tojo when already well into their professional practices in law and medicine. They returned after the war to a nation, America, and a region, southern California, where they were poised to inherit the world. Richard Nixon's ability to both embody and appeal to the new, ambitious leaders, in their Republican incarnation at least, defined much of the appeal that brought him to Congress as a representative of Orange County in 1946. In painting this portrait of the fall and recovery of a complex Nixon, Lungren has also provided a valuable self-portrait of a quintessential Nixon Man, a species that would, to the great consternation of liberals, come to define so much of American society by the last quarter of the twentieth century: conservatives, in a word.

It is instructive to hop back on the campaign train with

Nixon in 1952, 1954, 1956, 1958, 1960, and 1968. Some of the Lungrens' vignettes are familiar. ("Maybe this should be my last campaign," he tells his doctor—this time in 1954; but this was a lament that became semiannually familiar to many of his other intimates.) Other vignettes will be read by longtime Nixon-watchers with knowing smiles (or grimaces)—evidence of Nixon's skill at satisfying his underlings' sense of the boss's good intentions regarding decisions that were, in fact, considerably more complex. ("Jack," Nixon tells Lungren after sounding him out for information about John F. Kennedy's medical condition in 1960, "This is a personal subject and we will not use it in this campaign.") Many of the anecdotes are fresh and will satisfy those sympathetic to Nixon on the lookout for evidence of the sometimes less-than-pure intentions of the media regarding their treatment of their longtime bête noire—like the time Theodore White in 1960 was spotted wearing a JFK button on the Nixon campaign train and explained defensively that he was sticking with the winner, even though White was reporting to the public at the same time that it was Nixon, in fact, who was ahead at that point.

But the heart of the book is anguish. In the summer of 1974, the Watergate hearings were grinding inexorably towards impeachment, and Lungren, the friend and confidante, sent a telegram of support to his former charge. He received a surprising response five days later. A pain in his left leg, present in his last two presidential trips overseas, had grown worse. Nixon told Lungren it was his first illness since contracting childhood brucelosis because of his father's fetish for raw milk.

He asked Lungren to take over the treatment.

The invitation was an appeal of wounded vulnerability: "I want you to take care of me because I trust you," Nixon said, "and I know you wouldn't want anything from me." After the rough-and-tumble of a political lifetime, there were few people left he could trust. And what he said next, with "evident fear and anguish," showed more vulnerability still. "Jack, I will understand if you can't do it"—can't do it, that is, because of the ignominy and risk of public association with a disgraced and hated man.

"As I knew Nixon," Lungren then observes, "he was always able to cover up his inner feelings with energy and resilience. Nevertheless, this time I found Nixon very subdued." His "fear of dying was tangible and real, yet it was completely uncharacteristic of Nixon as I knew him." Hope dying, Nixon was bereft. Lungren was " truly worried about whether Nixon would recover."

Nixon's phlebitis grew worse. At one point, a leg clot blocked ninety-nine percent of his blood flow. At another point his blood pressure fell to 55/20. Lungren compares Nixon to King Lear (though Nixon himself, when he reads that description, increases the vulnerability factor by suggesting the example of Job instead), but this is more than a personal tragedy; this was a crucial and misunderstood era, stretching from the mid-1960s through the mid-1970s, when an aura of distrust and extremism suffused every side of every political question. It was an age of incompatible apocalyptic visions: where combatants shared an equal conviction that their way spelled righteousness and the way of the enemy was a threat to civilization itself. And many, right, left, and center, truly worried about whether the nation would recover.

It was a time when, for one side, it made perfect sense, when greeted with the announcement that the former President of the United States was too ill to function in public, to assume that it was a hoax. It came at a moment when suspicions were rampant that Gerald Ford only won the earliest possible succession to the presidency when Nixon promised to resign promptly in exchange for the unconditional pardon the president would soon give him. Even more urgently, it came at a moment when it looked inevitable that the former president would be hauled into court to testify before Judge John Sirica's criminal trial. The medical condition of the president, laid up in Southern California, would determine whether Nixon would testify. This book is never more vibrant than when recording the resulting drama.

Paranoia was everywhere. It was reported that Nixon was wearing pancake makeup upon his arrival at Long Beach Memorial Hospital Medical Center to make the staged scene play better on television. When Dr. Lungren took up duties as Nixon's liaison to the press, he was hit by a barrage of mouse-trapping questions insinuating that Nixon was not truly ill at all but was dodging Sirica's bullets instead. When Nixon was whisked back home to San Clemente according to Secret Service routine, an Associated Press reporter darkly intimated that the maneuver was "preserving the same secrecy which surrounded him at the White House." Watergate chief prosecutor James Neal accused Lungren of "stonewalling and protecting Nixon from testifying."

Dr. John Lungren had reasons to be suspicious as well, not least of which was the apparent burglary of his office and the copying of Nixon's medical records. And, being a quintessential Nixon Man, Dr. Lungren's resentment at Sirica's meddling takes the distinct and telling form of a regional bias that his work both analyzes and, for students of this neglected factor in America's political-cultural development, displays. Lungren's Long Beach Memorial

Hospital was the redoubt of young doctors who chose to establish their careers in the west because the more established and renowned institutions in the east and midwest were relatively closed to even the brightest newcomers, especially strivers without connections. The situation was, of course, identical for young lawyers like Nixon. The snubs they both experienced were real. So was the defensive pride western professionals built into their own counter-institutions. The chips that lingered on shoulders were real, too. You cannot understand Nixon and his men without understanding that. After Judge Sirica called a panel of "Eastern Medicine"[1] medical experts to confirm or contest Lungren's decision that Nixon was too ill to testify, the wounded "Westerner" angrily suggests to his patient, "Maybe we should ask the American Bar Association to appoint three Western federal judges to go to Washington and examine Judge Sirica." Lungren is Nixon's doctor indeed.

This account, though, offers more than just a sketch of the citizens inhabiting what historian Herbert Parmet would call "Nixon's America."[2] Dr. Lungren is also a skilled and empathetic man who was deeply worried about the health and resilience of the former president. All the human vulnerabilities kept piling up. Nixon's body was collapsing, and he was wracked by the indignities of political powerlessness. Embarking on his final flight to California after his resignation in the morning, Nixon reached "the edge of death, in dark psychological depression." It reminded Dr. Lungren of Churchill's words to his physician in 1955: "I'm waiting for death. But it won't come." Lungren made it his mission, as both physician and confidante, to help his charge avoid collapsing into terminal self-pity like some latter-day exiled Napoleon.

He proposed a regimen intended to draw Nixon out of

himself and back to himself—back to that man capable of drawing on inner iron to withstand great adversity, some of it self-inflicted, that would perhaps crush another. In this memoir Dr. Lungren writes that the longer he practiced medicine, the more he became convinced of "the mysterious, symbiotic unity of the mind and body, so fatefully interwoven"; he certainly found this true of Richard Nixon, and this unity forms the basis of the portrait he draws. Of all the many portraits of Nixon, none are more intimate than this one by Dr. Lungren—after all, his is "the most intimate and personal of professions."

Preface

John C. Lungren Jr.

MY FATHER DIED ON February 28, 2000. For five years in Laguna Niguel, California, from 1995 to his death, my father, John Charles Lungren, M.D., and I worked together as coauthors writing this book. Dad knew he was dying. Despite his illness, he sacrificed rest and comfort to finish the project he believed would rescue the inner life of Richard Nixon from oblivion—a retrieval of the full person as my father knew him.

As my father's final imperative, *Healing Richard Nixon: A Doctor's Memoir* was completed with the urgency and labor so essential to truth-telling and authenticity. I shared my father's urgency in completing this labor of intimate insight into a person whose achievements and failures continue to intrigue the nation. My father's relationship with Richard Nixon enabled him to explore the inner geography of a soul in mortal anguish. As Tom Wicker so aptly phrased it, Nixon is "one of us," capable of fortune or folly: "In the dark of their souls, which Nixon seems to have perceived, Americans could have seen in him themselves as they knew they were, not as they frequently dreamed of being."[1]

Living in Fair Oaks, California, near Sacramento, I would fly to southern California late Friday afternoon or early evening and spend the weekend with Dad to collaborate in the research and writing of the book. At 5:30 on Saturday mornings, I would hear a knock on the bedroom door. It would be Dad saying, "John, good morning. Did you sleep well? We need to get going on the book." Of course, Dad had been up since 5:00 or earlier, researching and writing on yellow legal pads, and was ready to discuss where we should proceed next in the manuscript. The authenticity of my father's voice is present throughout the narrative. In the writing of the book, I insisted that it was his voice, as clear as that knock on the door, that would resound and be heard.

In our collaboration, we intended for this memoir to provide wider service and perspective to the greater common purposes of the American nation and humanity. It was in the arena of the surpassing questions of life, history, and destiny that Nixon felt most at home and was most successful despite his human failings. My father and I believed what Richard Holmes has written about the transcendent nature of memoir and biography. Referring to Dr. Samuel Johnson's biography of Richard Savage, Holmes writes: "it began to pose the largest, imaginative questions: how well can we know our fellow human beings, how far can we learn from someone else's struggles about the condition of our own, what do the intimate circumstances of one particular life tell us about human nature in general?"[2]

My mother once told me: "I am a fortunate lady. Your father never said no to a house call." Now I do not think that mother meant she was fortunate because Dad was out of the house and not underfoot. What my mother meant was that the house calls were symbolic of the commitment to health and well-being that compassionate, caring physicians bring to their patients, their patients' families, and the larger communities of city, state, nation, and world. The physician revives, restores, and heals the whole person, a priest-like calling most evident in my father's life. How many patients' lives did he revive, restore, and heal? How many did he ease into the final passages of life? Rich and poor alike, from president to plumber, there was broad compassion; all were treated with equal dignity. When Richard Nixon needed my father's care and confidence as a physician and friend, my father responded with profound empathy for his patient, who was suffering great travail of body and spirit.

Empathy for the whole person is the undying legacy of humane care and practice my father left to his beloved medical profession, for he was one of those physicians with a legendary bedside manner who shared and guided his patients through the course of their lives, as Reynolds Price has recalled. "Those doctors never indulged in false consolations," Price observed.[3] For Richard Nixon, there was never false consolation from my father, only the balm of grace and truth. What was written about Lord Moran, Churchill's personal physician, could also be written about my father: "His skill in diagnosis and the unhesitating speed with which he found the right men at the right time were the greatest services he rendered."[4]

My father and Richard Nixon embodied that cardinal passion for life most manifest in deep affection for their professions, medicine and politics. Both believed in professions which are directed to creating and preserving the greater social good. Moreover, both were possessed by the soul's eternal quest: What does the Creator expect of us? For myself, I was given a rare gift—the intense collaboration with my father during the final five years of his life. Sons usually have their most intense experiences with their fathers at a very young age. I was privileged to have it later in life.

Fathers and sons! What love and solidarity coexist in the majesty of that ancient bond.

Preface

John C. Lungren, M.D.

RICHARD NIXON WAS SUBJECT TO the most rigorous scrutiny conceivable from both the media and the public during the course of his political and private life. Yet he remains a misunderstood and enigmatic figure. To many, Nixon seems a paradox—a man of contradictory impulses and incongruous actions whom critics and observers have never been able to fathom. As his personal physician, I had the opportunity to observe the astonishing life and political career of Richard Nixon at close range for more than forty years. I saw him in triumph and defeat, under extreme stress, in the depths of depression, and even close to death.

The purpose of this book is to present both a physician and friend's perspective of Richard Nixon and to give a more humane and comprehensive insight into this complex man whom I came to know through confidential and privileged observation, conversation, and dialogue for four decades. To achieve such completeness, the ethics of medicine and demands of candor compelled me to secure a complete legal release from the former president. As a physician practicing the most intimate and personal of professions, I could not write a complete memoir without such permission. Physicians live by a unique standard of ethics—the practice of medicine is an art and a science which preserves and protects the ultimate privacy between physician and patient.

Richard Nixon in both a legal document and a handwritten note on a scrap of old stationery gave me the permission and the encouragement to delineate the real "RN." Both documents were signed on December 21, 1975, seventeen months and thirteen days after his resignation, while he was in exile at his home La Casa Pacifica in San Clemente, California. The first document is an executed, typed legal instrument signed "Richard M. Nixon":

> Being advised of Dr. John C. Lungren's proposal to publish a book including in part my medical history and his account of our past 25 years of friendship, I welcome the opportunity to authorize Dr. Lungren to state and reproduce, without reservation, any and all facts, matters and documentation in any manner relating to my medical history and our friendship which he may have knowledge. This does not constitute an endorsement of any of the contents of the work, but is intended to release Dr. Lungren from all the ethical restraints which would otherwise encumber his presentation of a fair and accurate report.
>
> Richard M. Nixon

The second document is written in Nixon's inimitable, propulsive, and right-slanted cursive, which always gave me the impression of a mind in motion:

Jack—

I think your forward [*sic*] is excellent—
    I would suggest only one small change. The
reference to Lear would be understood only by a
few Shakespeare scholars. Job—might be a better
Name. More people read the Bible than
Shakespeare (I hope!) Perhaps another more
common word—giant or (you choose it) would
be better—
    In any event many thanks for undertaking this
project—
    Hit *hard*—with all the facts! RN
    [over]
    I suggest you read the Introduction to my book *Six
Crises*—
    to get an idea of the philosophy which has
sustained me—

    RN

    Although I initially began to write this book in 1975, I
came to the conclusion that any memoir of my relationship with Richard Nixon would not be truly comprehensive and compelling until after his death. Fearing the
unfinished narrative, Hamlet instructs his friend Horatio
to "report me and my cause aright to the unsatisfied."[5] Was
Nixon suggesting the same to me in his note? In requesting that I substitute Job or "giant" for King Lear was Nixon
telling me that, like Job, he would overcome anguish and
fear, ultimately achieving wisdom and a final peace? When
Nixon thanked me for initiating the project, and then told
me to use all of the facts vigorously, was he tacitly intimat-

ing that I should—like Horatio—report his "cause" to the "unsatisfied"? To the unsatisfied I will report the unadorned Nixon as I knew him: impassioned, guarded, intellectual, introverted, disciplined, emotional, brilliant, deeply religious, and tragic.

I recall the penultimate paragraph of *Six Crises* in which Nixon described a private conversation he had with Charles de Gaulle. While visiting the United States in 1960, De Gaulle had told Nixon that he had the rare privilege to enjoy some of his greatest days late in life. He quoted Sophocles, who wrote that "one must wait until the evening to see how splendid the day has been."[6] I had the rare privilege of observing both the anguish and the splendor of Richard Nixon's days and nights. I will relate them with the candor and compassion of a physician and friend—ever-mindful of the intermingling of joy and sorrow that fills all our days and nights.

Acknowledgments

The following persons provided invaluable encouragement, counsel, and support in the preparation of this book: David L. Lungren, Daniel E. Lungren, Erin K. Lungren, Nancy Jean Lungren, Susan Naulty, and Dorothy O'Connor. Thank you very much.

But I have found that leaders are subject to all
the human frailties . . .

—Richard Nixon
Six Crises

When the Pacific called out the response of his
united body and mind, he wrote the enduring
signature of his age. He gives full expression to
its abundance, to its energetic desire to master
history by repossessing all the resources of the
hidden past in a timeless and heroic present.
But he did not avoid the darkness in that past,
the perpetual suffering in the heart of man, the
broken arc of his career which inevitably ends
in death.

—F.O. Matthiessen on Melville
American Renaissance

Outside this room the chill of grace
Lies heavy on the morning grass.

—Alice Goodman, librettist
Nixon in China

1

The Cease of Majesty

IT WAS HIS SEVENTH AND FINAL CRISIS. Like Dante, he had descended into hell. Whether Richard Nixon would return was unknown to him, to God, and to me, his personal physician. On Thursday, August 8, 1974, at 9:00 P.M., Richard Milhous Nixon addressed his fellow citizens from the White House for sixteen excruciating minutes. Concealing inner dread, the thirty-seventh president of the United States uttered a sentence never before pronounced in two centuries of the American republic: "Therefore, I shall resign the Presidency effective at noon tomorrow." When he finished speaking, the president, exhausted, anguished, and limping slightly, walked to the private family living quarters in the White House, where he "started to shake violently."[1] Unfolding its insidious course, Watergate had destroyed Nixon's presidency with savage, unrelenting force. A tangled web of deceit subverted truth, undermined institutional integrity, and paralyzed the government.

At home in California, a continent away, I watched with my family as President Nixon delivered his televised resignation speech from the Oval Office. I felt deep sorrow at the president's woeful fall and tragic disgrace, the public trauma and horrid waste of Watergate.

I knew that a political vacuum would ensue, the most precarious time in a democracy. I knew that bitter recriminations would rupture, flowing like contaminated blood into American political life with Watergate joining the Vietnam War in a dangerous intermingling. I knew that President Nixon's vision of forging a new international balance of power for a generation of peace would probably be lost beyond recovery. I knew that Nixon himself would suffer the torment, alienation, and the banishment of psychological and political exile. Nevertheless, those unprecedented ten words of resignation pronounced by President Nixon also set in motion a drama of redemption in which I would become a principal protagonist and witness. I was propelled onto a dramatic stage where history, politics, medicine, and the media encountered the forces of destiny.

I was in the ruinous wake of Watergate, where trepidation and disquiet dwelled. There I found the former president of the United States in physical and psychological trauma and the American nation suffering a great civic tragedy. I was charged with returning the banished Richard Nixon to the republic, whole and restored. What follows is the story of his anguish and ultimate redemption.

At the zenith of power and acclaim, President Nixon abandoned wise advisers and directed a cover-up of the Watergate break-in at the Democratic National Headquarters in June 1972. The president executed orders to buy the silence of the arrested burglars and directed the CIA to thwart the FBI investigation. Nixon doomed himself by preserving his own incriminating words on the voice-activated recording system in the Oval Office, an act of self-inflicted harm so devastating that it continues to astonish us.[2]

On July 27, 1974, the House Judiciary Committee voted articles of impeachment. Nixon faced an impeachment vote in the House and, if impeached, a trial in the Senate as well as a total erosion of the political support he needed to govern as president. A day earlier, I had sent Nixon a telegram encouraging him by saying I was praying for him and his family to withstand this terrible ordeal. To my amazement, I received a personal note from the president, signed "RN" and postmarked only eight days before his resignation speech. That he could even remember my telegram, much less respond rationally under the circumstances, remains a testament to his fortitude and tenacity:

August 1, 1974

Dear Jack:

It is typical of you to always do the right thing at the right time, and I deeply appreciate your thoughtful telegram of July 26. Your words of friendship and concern mean more than I can say, and they are a source strength and encouragement for me at this difficult time.
Pat joins me in sending our warmest good wishes to Lorain and you.

RN

As revelations of Nixon's involvement in the Watergate cover-up continued day by day, I experienced the disturbing pity, sorrow, and dread an audience feels in viewing classical tragedy. Nixon perceived his fate as inevitable: "more than once over the next days I would yield to my desire to fight, and I would bridle as the inexorable end drew near."[3] Forever grasped in memory is my initial encounter with Richard Nixon twenty-two years before that dark August evening of his resignation. I first met him on his campaign train before it left Pomona, California, for the Golden State's Great Central Valley on September 17, 1952. It was a bright, warm, fall afternoon in Pomona, known for its lemon and orange groves, near the foothills of the San Gabriel Mountains east of Los Angeles. Nixon was starting a whistle-stop campaign as the Republican vice presidential candidate. Hundreds of supporters were crowding around the rear of the Santa Fe El Capitan with its great diesel engines painted in the famous red, yellow, black, and silver war-bonnet design and renamed the Dick Nixon Special. I boarded the candidate's El Capitan Pullman car and was directed to his private compartment by my friend Jack Drown, a lawyer and businessman who was acting as campaign train manager. Drown opened the door and introduced me to Senator Nixon, his wife Pat, and campaign manager Murray Chotiner. Nixon and I exchanged greetings and proceeded to have a brief yet substantive conversation about the campaign.

My first impression of Nixon was that he was a rather young man for a United States senator. Like many Americans, I had followed his meteoric career at a distance since he left the Navy after World War II, was elected to Congress, achieved national prominence in the Alger Hiss case, and defeated Helen Gahagan Douglas in 1951 in a bitterly fought campaign for the Senate. He was relatively youthful at thirty-nine years of age, but I noted a seriousness of purpose and focused alacrity of mind. During this brief encounter, I realized that his highly visible rise to prominence would not be a short-lived, transitory phenomenon.

In 1952, I was thirty-six years old and married to Lorain Youngberg; we had four of our seven children. I was born in Sioux City, Iowa, on April 27, 1916, delivered to the American midwest as the only child of a Swedish-Lutheran father, Charles Lungren, and an Irish-Catholic mother, Julia Murphy, who bore me when she was forty years of age.

Charles Lungren was a second-generation immigrant who was born in Boston soon after his parents arrived in America from Sweden. His parents, who were extremely poor, emigrated to Alta, Iowa, where grandfather Lungren worked as a blacksmith and tried to invent a perpetual-motion machine. Knowing that his parents could not afford high school, my father decided to go through the eighth grade twice. He became a stock boy in a wholesale drug house, studied at a pharmacy school, and passed the state pharmacy boards.

My father moved to Sioux City, where he met my mother Julia, a graduate of Iowa State Normal, the state teachers' college. The great potato famine of the 1840s had driven my mother's family from Ireland to Nebraska, where the Murphy men were railroad engineers. My father founded a chain of drugstores in Sioux City, became ill with heart disease, and retired early. He then moved our family west to California, golden land of promise, searching for a better climate to redress his heart condition and raise his only son.

I spent my early formative years in a Catholic grammar and high school, St. Anthony, in Long Beach, California. After my father died, when I was fourteen years old, my mother and I returned to Sioux City where I finished high school. After graduating from the University of Notre Dame in 1938, I received a medical degree from the University of Pennsylvania Medical School four years later. (I specialized in internal medicine and cardiology and passed my board examinations in each field to become a Fellow of the American College of Internal Medicine and the American College of Cardiology.)

While interning at Los Angles County Hospital, I met

Lorain Kathleen Youngberg on a blind date. She was a beautiful and beguiling former New York fashion and photographer's model at John Robert Powers, the famous modeling school and agency, and was an aspiring actress. My future wife was born and raised in Chicago, descended from second-generation Swedish and Irish immigrants. I married Lorain Kathleen on June 15, 1943, in the uniform of a first lieutenant in the United States Army Medical Corps.

Serving in the army during World War II as a battalion surgeon in the 30th Infantry Division, I experienced the carnage of war during the Normandy landing and at the pivotal battles of Saint-Lo and Mortain. I received a Purple Heart and four Battle Stars for wounds suffered near Mortain. I was hospitalized in Paris, returned to active duty as a captain in the army medical corps, and concluded my overseas military service as battalion surgeon in Frankfurt am Main after it had been liberated by the allies. Upon my return in 1945, I saw the child born during my time overseas—our son John.

My experience during World War II led me to the conviction that the danger of war increases when a generation forfeits strong and effective political leadership through apathy and indifference. Hitler's rise to power was never challenged by effective political opposition and the Japanese never had a viable political counterweight to their military establishment.

In 1952, with the Korean War raging, I was attracted to Nixon because he too had experienced the unchallenged aggression of Germany and Japan that had resulted in the deaths of tens of millions. Nixon not only had experienced war, but he appeared to know how to outmaneuver aggressors with a strong defense strategy and effective political calculation.

In July at the Republican National Convention in Chicago, General Dwight D. Eisenhower selected Nixon as his running mate. When I heard that Nixon had been chosen, I was pleased that he was on the ticket with Eisenhower—providing a good balance of maturing youth and mature war hero. I did not realize, however, that only two months later on that Santa Fe Pullman car in Pomona, I would begin a friendship with Richard Nixon that would last more than four decades and transform my own life as an American physician and citizen in the second half of the twentieth century.

When Jack Drown asked me and two Long Beach, California, medical colleagues, Dr. Malcolm Todd and Dr. Hubert Pritchard, to act as volunteer campaign physicians, I accepted without reservation. We would stagger our vacation schedules in three-week segments so that each of us would cover a portion of the nine-week campaign from September through election day in November.

2

From Pharaohs to Phlebitis

IN THE TURBULENT AFTERMATH of the resignation, on two occasions in late August and early September 1974, Dr. Walter Tkach, Nixon's White House physician, contacted me by telephone. Major General Tkach was a career U.S. Air Force physician who had been assigned to the White House when Nixon became president. My relationship with him was highly professional. Dr. Tkach was a caring physician who served the White House well during the Nixon years.

Dr. Tkach had called me because he was seriously concerned about the former president's health. He described the swollen condition of Nixon's left leg and asked me to drive to San Clemente and examine him. I agreed, and he said that he would make the necessary arrangements. He tried to do this on two occasions. However, on both occasions, Dr. Tkach called back to tell me that he had failed to get Nixon's permission. Nixon was in no mood for visitors. According to Robert Sam Anson, those who did see him reported that Nixon "look ravaged"—his "eyes were red-rimmed and hollow," and during conversations he "snapped" at people.[1]

Nixon was furious with the Ford White House. President Ford's senior staff was treating Nixon as a pariah in terms of moving his personal papers, authorizing intelligence briefings, permitting the use of military aircraft, and granting other perquisites and courtesies available to former presidents. There was even serious discussion by the Ford staff of charging Nixon for the post-resignation part of *Air Force One*'s flight returning Nixon to California. Nixon was angry and frustrated, telling an aide that as a former president he was "entitled to anything that any other former president is entitled to. . . . I expect to be treated the same way. When I travel, I expect military aircraft; I expect the same support I provided. I expect communications and medical personnel, everything they had. And, goddam it, you tell Ford I expect it."[2] Nixon's resignation became effective at twelve noon eastern daylight time, August 9, 1974, when Gerald Ford was sworn in as the nation's thirty-eighth president. At that moment, *Air Force One* was thirteen miles southwest of Jefferson City, Missouri, flying at thirty-nine thousand feet.[3]

In the tumultuous wake of Nixon's resignation, there was one overwhelming subject that dominated every discussion of his future: pardon or indictment? Bryce Harlow, Nixon's former chief liaison with Congress, supported a pardon, contending forcefully that a trial would create emotional division and political schism in America, the bitter recriminations that I had believed would surely occur after Nixon resigned.[4] Secretary of State Henry Kissinger supported a pardon for two reasons. He argued that a trial of the former president would be "gravely damaging" to United States prestige abroad, and he predicted that Nixon could not physically or psychologically survive an indictment and trial.[5]

Leonard Garment, counsel to the president, asked former Supreme Court Justice Abe Fortas, a liberal justice and close adviser to President Johnson, whether Nixon should be pardoned. Fortas replied that it was time for reconciliation—"Ecclesiastes time"—not retribution.[6] The writer of Ecclesiastes, one of the Bible's great books of mercy, petitions the Creator for an assuaging wisdom: "Wisdom makes the wise stronger than a dozen governors in a city. No one on earth is sufficiently upright to do good without ever sinning."[7]

On August 29, Garment sent a memorandum to Chief of Staff Alexander Haig outlining the reasons why President Ford should extend a full pardon to Nixon. Attached to the memorandum was a compelling draft of a pardon statement for President Ford written by Nixon's chief speechwriter, Ray Price.Watergate-related matters were taking up three-quarters of President Ford's time. Nixon was receiving subpoenas from the Justice Department relating to Watergate criminal actions. Soon, Watergate prosecutors would focus on indicting Nixon. President Ford was concerned that a criminal trial of Nixon would tear the nation apart with legal complexities and political recriminations.[8]

In the pardon statement President Ford declared that the Constitution, despite its supremacy clause, is surpassed by a higher order of jurisprudence—"the laws of God, which govern our consciences." He elevated the issue of Nixon's pardon above the realm of law and the Constitution into the higher spheres of conscience, mercy, and the forgiveness of a forbearing community: "I do believe, with all my heart and mind and spirit, that I, not as President but as a humble servant of God, will receive justice without mercy if I fail to show mercy. Finally, I feel that Richard Nixon and his loved ones have suffered enough and will continue to suffer, no matter what we, as a great and good nation, can do together to make his goal of peace come true."[9]

Many political observers now believe that President Ford's pardon, somewhat neglected until recently by historians and journalists, was one of those rare political acts done in the spirit of forgiveness, such as General MacArthur's redemptive restoration of Japan.

President Ford pardoned Richard Nixon on September 8, 1974, exactly one month after Nixon's resignation speech. President Ford's pardon was an act of both moral conscience and pragmatic politics. He needed a rapid political closure to Nixon's resignation so that he could govern effectively. He also needed to ensure that the former president would receive mercy as well as justice and not be pursued with abandon by prosecutors. On May 27, 2001, President Ford received the Profile in Courage award from the John F. Kennedy Library for his pardon of President Nixon.

On September 11, 1974, three days after President Ford pardoned Nixon, I received an early-evening telephone call from Palm Desert, California. The call was from U.S. Marine Colonel Jack Brennan, Nixon's military aide: "Doctor Lungren," said Brennan with some urgency, "the Boss's left leg is worse. He wants to see you."

Nixon was then resting at Ambassador Walter Annenberg's estate in Palm Desert. A generous philanthropist, Annenberg was U.S. Ambassador to Great Britain under Nixon. Annenberg had parlayed his father's publishing business (*TV Guide*, the *Racing Form*) into great wealth—the fruits of which included his Palm Desert estate, complete with a private golf course.

A former career Marine officer, Colonel Brennan had been Nixon's military aide in the White House and was serving as his chief of staff and principal assistant. He managed Nixon's office at San Clemente and accompanied him wherever he went. Serving in Vietnam before being assigned to the White House in 1968, the swarthy Brennan had been wounded in battle and awarded a Purple Heart and a commendation for leadership and heroism. Colonel Brennan, always loyal and dedicated, had supervised presidential ceremonies, protocol, and travel for Nixon in the White House, visiting fifty countries, including Russia and China. Brennan's loyalty to Nixon went far beyond duty. He was extremely protective of Nixon and acutely understood—and felt—Nixon's profound anguish at resigning the presidency.

Brennan insisted: "Doctor, I know it's late, and a long drive, but could you possibly come out to Ambassador Annenberg's tonight and see the president? I am very concerned. The Boss really needs you as he never did." "Of course, I'll come right away. I'll leave for Palm Desert as soon as I finish seeing my patients," I replied.

I left Long Beach at 8:30 P.M. and arrived in the desert community two hours later. I called Colonel Brennan from a Palms Springs service station, and he directed me to follow Highway 111 through Palms Springs to Palm Desert. When I reached the corner of Bob Hope Drive and Frank Sinatra Drive, following Brennan's instructions, I turned left and looked to the right for an abandoned service station where an unmarked white Plymouth sedan was parked with its lights out. As I drove into the empty station, the white Plymouth's lights flashed on and off several times by prearranged signal. A Secret Service agent stepped out of the car and demanded my identification. I followed the Plymouth down Frank Sinatra Drive to the Annenberg estate, which we entered through the rear security gate.

I was greeted by Brennan, Nixon's valet, Manola Sanchez, and several Secret Service agents. Before being taken to Nixon's private quarters, I was called to the telephone. A White House operator was on the line. "Dr. Lungren? Yes, thank you. Please hold for Admiral Lukash," the operator said.

Admiral William Lukash, President Ford's White House physician, had been the assistant White House physician under Dr. Tkach during the Nixon Administration. We had an extensive conversation about the origin of Nixon's leg problems.

Lukash came on the line: "I am so glad and relieved I reached you. We have been quite concerned since just before President Nixon left for the Middle East to see Sadat. That's when the leg really started to get worse. The president hid it from us until we were well on our way to Cairo. He told me in Salzburg of the leg's rapid swelling. I examined him immediately and diagnosed it as acute phlebitis in the lower left leg."

"Did it get worse in Egypt?" I asked.

"Yes, exactly. The president refused to sit down and rest his leg on the rear platform of the open coach during the train ride from Cairo to Alexandria with President Sadat. He remained standing next to Sadat as if he intended for every Egyptian and the entire Middle East to see this alliance. The longer he stood, the more intense the pain grew. He suffered an acute flare-up in the leg and I placed him on anti-inflammatory drugs," Lukash reported.

Nixon's existing condition had clearly been aggravated by his extensive foreign travel in June 1974 when he had made his last two foreign trips as president—to Egypt and to the Soviet Union. He traveled to Egypt to visit President Anwar al-Sadat, whose peace initiatives were gaining momentum. Nixon was determined to restore the balance of power in the Middle East. On June 9, three days before leaving for Egypt, he wrote in his diary: "All I must do is to do everything possible to see that we leave a structure on which future Presidents can build—a structure built on military strength, diplomatic sophistication, intelligence, and, of course, a strong strain of idealism."[10]

By this time, Watergate was pressing inexorably down on Nixon. In Salzburg, where the presidential party had stopped overnight to adjust to the change in time on the way to Cairo, Secretary of State Kissinger held a press conference. He threatened to resign over a *New York Times* editorial accusing him of not giving forthright testimony to the Senate Committee concerning wiretaps in 1969.[11]

While in Salzburg, Nixon wrote in his diary: "I felt good this morning except for the fact that my left leg is having exactly the same symptoms it had when I was in Hawaii and had what was diagnosed as a blood clot. I am having Lukash come over and look at it since he was one who measured it before. It is much larger than the right leg and it really makes me quite lame. I, of course, will not allow them to do anything which will disrupt the trip at this point."[12]

Nixon received a hero's welcome in Cairo, where he was greeted by emotional crowds of one hundred deep along the motorcade route and an estimated total of over a million people. The next day Nixon and Sadat traveled from Cairo to Alexandria by train, amid even larger crowds. The three-hour trip was exhausting as Nixon and Sadat stood at the back of an open coach waving to the crowds, and they also held a news conference.

In continuing to bring me up to date, Lukash reported that after Nixon returned to Washington from Egypt, the leg seemed to improve and the president refused any further treatment. Lukash noted that later in June, however, when Nixon flew to Russia for a summit with Leonid Brezhnev, "the leg began flaring up once more."

"How aware is the president of the risks involved?" I asked. "The president is aware that the condition is potentially fatal. I told him that a blood clot could break loose, travel through the veins from the infected leg to the lungs, triggering a deadly pulmonary embolus," Lukash explained.

He continued, "Dr. Lungren, you don't know how relieved we are that you are going to examine the president now. Please, call me after you have made your diagnosis despite the late hour, so I can keep President Ford informed." The tenor of Admiral Lukash's remarks provided evidence of not only his deep concern but the concern of President Ford as well.

The Secret Service then escorted me to Nixon's quarters, a well-appointed guest bungalow that included a bedroom and a large living room with a private entrance. Colonel Brennan brought me into the living room, where Nixon greeted me; he was seated on a large stuffed chair with the affected left leg elevated on the ottoman.

"Jack, how are you? Glad to see you."

"'I'm fine—but the important thing is how you are," I replied.

Colonel Brennan took leave of us. Nixon then confided anxiously, "Jack, I really need your help. I want you to take care of me because I trust you, and I know you don't want anything from me." Nixon paused for a moment, adding, "I will understand if you can't do it."

"Remember, Dick, we have been close friends for twenty-five years, and I am confident we will conquer this crisis as we have in the past," I assured him.

Nixon looked exhausted; he was pale and had obviously lost considerable weight. Drawn and tense, he was dressed in blue pajamas, a blue robe, and black slippers. Despite his apparent exhaustion, however, his voice was as strong as ever. While his penetrating intellect seemed intact, there was also fear and anguish that I had never seen in him before. I had never observed such trauma and torment during any of his enumerated "six crises," from Alger Hiss to Nikita Khrushchev to John F. Kennedy to his notorious "last press conference" in 1962, or even to the death in September 1967 of his beloved mother Hannah. This time it was different; it was fear and anguish so profound that I discerned that a vital part of Nixon was close to being lost forever, something so uprooted in his inner self that his will to live was endangered. I thought Nixon had behaved rationally for a man who had suffered the anguish, torment, and ultimate disgrace of resigning the presidency. Yet my overall impression was that he was profoundly depressed. I did not detect very much of his old fighting spirit. The Nixon I had known was always able to conceal his inner feelings with energy and resilience, but this time I found Nixon very subdued.

I pulled up a chair opposite the ottoman and immediately inquired about the history of the phlebitis. Nixon told me that the lower left leg had been swollen since early June. What worried him now was that he had developed considerable pain in the left calf muscle. He said that he was sorry I had to make such a long trip so late at night but for the first time he was really worried about the leg.

Following a routine physical examination with particular attention to the lower left leg, I found that he had chronic active phlebitis with a possible extension into the deep venous system of the upper left thigh. I also reminded him of Dr. Lukash's warning—the danger of the possible formation of a blood clot in the leg, which could travel to the lungs and cause the fatal blood-clotting of a pulmonary embolism. I strongly recommended immediate hospitalization and anticoagulation (blood-thinning) therapy.

Nixon was adamant and unyielding. "No," he declared fearfully, "If I go to the hospital, I'll never come out alive."

Nixon's fear of dying was great, and yet it was completely uncharacteristic of the Nixon I had known. Instead of resilience and hope, I detected the deep despair, anguish, and mental torment manifest in his face and voice. Hope dying, Nixon was bereft. It reminded me of the anxiety that often overwhelms patients who are suffering a fatal disease. When I see patients in this state, I know that they are reviewing their life, dwelling on last things, suffering great depression of mind and soul. It is a kind of foreclosure on life. In this context, I was truly worried whether Nixon would recover.

"I can't force you go to the hospital. But I will prescribe medication for your use here at home. This may be of some help, but is highly inadequate and cannot substitute for the hospital," I answered. I prescribed an anticoagulant and an anti-inflammatory drug, bed rest, and elevation of the leg. We agreed that I would reexamine the leg in a few days in San Clemente.

Following the examination, we moved to a recreation room, and Nixon mixed each of us a scotch-and-soda, his usual, single drink. As we were conversing, he commented on the Notre Dame–Georgia Tech football game he had seen on television a few days earlier. Nixon said he was very impressed by the speed, passing, and leadership of Notre Dame's quarterback, Tom Clements. Clements had led Notre Dame to a now-famous victory over Bear Bryant's Alabama team for the national championship in the January 1973 Sugar Bowl. I made a mental note that Nixon's remarkable knowledge and love of sports had not been extinguished by the ordeal of resignation and Watergate. I always looked for such enthusiasm and interest in seriously ill patients, for it was a sign of inner resilience and will.

By this time, it was 12:30 A.M. Nixon urged me to stay overnight, as did his longtime and loyal valet, Manola Sanchez. However, I declined because I had many patients at Long Beach Memorial Hospital, and I needed to make early-morning hospital rounds. Two Secret Service agents escorted me in their unmarked car as far as San Bernardino.

As I drove home, I reflected that President Ford's pardon of Nixon, while preventing prosecution, did not assuage Nixon's inner anguish and would not stop the progressive worsening of his physical condition, psychological exile, and social banishment.

3

Dread Unconcealed

AT 3:00 P.M. ON SEPTEMBER 16, I arrived at La Casa Pacifica as previously scheduled to reexamine the former president. I was greeted by Manola Sanchez, who led me to the swimming pool area. Here I found Nixon, casually dressed and seated at the edge of the pool in a chaise lounge with his left leg elevated. Pat Nixon was sitting beside him.

We exchanged greetings, and I asked about the leg. "I believe the damn leg is worse—more pain and swelling," he said. He appeared irritable and depressed, and the left leg was painful to pressure. I insisted that he be hospitalized. Fortunately, Julie Nixon Eisenhower was visiting her father. With his daughter standing beside me, I once again tried to persuade Nixon to enter the hospital, saying, "Dick, now that Julie, probably your most ardent supporter, and your longtime friend and physician agree, would you let me call Long Beach Memorial to make the necessary arrangements for admission?"

Nixon answered, "How can I not say yes? Go ahead and call." I went to the telephone, reached the admitting office, and arranged for his admission on the following Monday.

On Monday, September 23, Nixon traveled in a small

21

motorcade from San Clemente to Long Beach. He was accompanied by Pat, Julie Eisenhower, his former press secretary Ronald L. Ziegler, and four Secret Service agents. For security reasons, Nixon arrived at the rear loading dock of the hospital. The Secret Service dictated the circumstances of his entry to protect him and his family. These security measures were necessary and routine. They were not taken to hide his whereabouts as was later suggested by staff writers at the *Long Beach Independent Press-Telegram*: "Although security seemed lax when the former president entered the Long Beach medical facility, by Friday a giant wall was built between newsmen and any shred of information. There have been three official answers to newsmen's questions. 'I don't know,' 'I can't answer that,' and 'I'll see if I can find out.'"[1]

As Nixon emerged from the Lincoln limousine, I asked him how he felt. He whispered to me in a low voice: "Jack, the leg is even worse. The pain and swelling have traveled up to my thigh." Nixon appeared depressed and weak; he had a sallow complexion and an unsteady gait. Nevertheless, he walked without assistance to the service elevator, which brought us to the sixth floor of the hospital. During the elevator ride, I could not help but vividly recall the last time Richard Nixon had visited Long Beach Memorial Hospital. It had been on January 2, 1969, three weeks before his inauguration as the thirty-seventh president of the United States. In a mere five years and nine months, this man at my side, a patient and friend, had experienced untold elation, triumph, disgrace, and ignominy—a compressed and anguished odyssey. As the elevator rose, poignant images flashed through my mind. I had a vivid recollection of January 2, 1969. The president-elect had come to my office for a physical examination. The hospital and my office had spent several days in preparation for his arrival. The hospital parking lot had been cleared and secured as a landing pad for the presidential helicopter. The Secret Service had come to my office and the hospital several days before to reconnoiter and to secure every inch of the path Nixon would take. Secure phone lines were installed; security background checks of hospital staff were made; diagrams of my private office, interior corridors, and rooms were sketched and disseminated among the Secret Service agents.

On the morning of January 2, the white-canopied, olive-green presidential helicopter, what was to become *Marine One* for President Nixon—the same one that was to carry him out of office 2,066 days later—descended in all its majesty to a cordoned-off parking lot near my medical office. The whirring blades slowed to a stop. I greeted the president-elect as he descended the helicopter stairway. We entered a waiting presidential limousine for the short journey to the rear entrance of my office building. An entourage of staff, his military aide Colonel Don Hughes, and Secret Service agents followed.

In the limousine, I reminded Nixon that our last meeting had been after the election in New York City at the Waldorf-Astoria ballroom in the early morning hours following his victory speech. I thought to myself that this morning Nixon looked even more exuberant and triumphant, ready to assume the presidency with vibrant physical resilience and intellectual energy.

At the completion of my physical examination, I pronounced him to be in excellent health and ready to assume the challenges of the presidency. I then escorted him on an inspection tour of the hospital. It was a triumphal visit. Nixon was greeted with much enthusiasm by the patients, staff, and all the visitors. We then proceeded to the major conference room. I introduced him to an audience that included the board of directors of the hospital and the leaders of the medical staff. Nixon delivered his address without notes, as I had seen him do on many occasions.

Nixon warned that a great battle would soon be waged over the future of privately financed medical services. "The real test over the next decade will be if this kind of a private medical institution can survive and whether the individual doctor-patient relationship will survive," he declared. At the conclusion of his remarks, I accompanied the him to *Marine One*. We were mobbed by a large crowd of applauding onlookers and a phalanx of television crews and reporters. We shook hands, and Nixon climbed the helicopter steps, turned, waved to the crowd, and gave his familiar two-handed victory gesture with extended index and middle fingers forming V's.

No clairvoyant or Cassandra could have predicted that Nixon would end his presidency in a mournful mirror image of that auspicious departure from Long Beach Memorial eighteen days before his inauguration in January 1969. Refracted by folly, the final reflection became a fading double image, a distorted duplication of Nixon's triumphant arrivals and departures in the great cities of the world—London, Paris, Rome, Warsaw, Moscow, Cairo, and Beijing.

On that January morning in 1969, having pronounced the president-elect physically and mentally fit to assume the highest office of the world's most powerful nation, I could never have imagined the inexhaustibly sad, final coda that was to come five and a half years later for Richard Nixon on Friday, August 9, 1974. I could never have conceived that I would see my friend and patient Richard Nixon in this profoundly weakened and demoralized condition and would begin a long effort to heal his pain, anguish, and grief.

When the service elevator jerked to a stop on the sixth floor, my reminiscence ceased, and I looked over at the former president and saw a man torn asunder by a grave physical illness and the debilitating mental anguish of having been the only president ever to resign his office. I felt a great sadness over what Watergate had wrought and compassion for my friend and patient brought to this abject condition.

The elevator door opened. A hospital orderly waiting with a wheelchair took Nixon to a private room in the sixth-floor west wing. This wing was cordoned off for use by Nixon, his wife and family, and the Secret Service.

I conducted a physical examination, observing that Nixon had lost additional weight and had a gaunt look but that he retained his mental alertness. In fact, I judged his mental acuity to be excellent. When I examined the left leg, I found it to be enlarged from the toes to the hip. It was tender to touch, markedly so over the calf, which was indicative of a possible clot. I ordered an intravenous drip of Heparin, an anticlotting drug.

I met Pat Nixon and Julie Eisenhower in an adjoining room and advised them of my diagnosis, its seriousness, and the need for intensified treatment. I assured them that I believed this hospital stay with the treatment ordered would result in real improvement. They responded with great concern but with their emotions under control.

After I left the room, Ron Ziegler told me that Nixon and his family wanted me to make a brief statement about his condition to the press. Accompanied by Ziegler, I went to the first-floor conference room where I was met by fifty to seventy-five reporters and cameramen. A podium and microphone were set up in the front of the room. Ziegler spoke first, giving a short description of the day's events and announcing that daily written medical statements would be released. Ziegler introduced me, and I stepped to the podium.

I spoke very briefly about Nixon's condition and the ethical ground rules I would follow:

> Ladies and gentlemen, I am here to issue a statement with regard to President Nixon's hospitalization. At the outset may I say that this session and any other press releases that might follow will be conducted within the code of the patient-doctor relationship. Accordingly, such issues as progress and treatment, medication usage, new developments, all will be reported first to the patient, then to his wife and immediate family, and then with their permission, a statement may be made.
>
> I have just examined Mr. Nixon again; understandably, he exhibits evidence of physical fatigue. Mr. Nixon's hospital admission has a two-fold purpose. Number one, to treat a chronic phlebitis, an acute phase which first developed on his trip to the Middle East, and which has already had three episodes of reactivation. The treatment will consist primarily of the introduction of the prophylactic use of anticoagulation drugs, and to conduct exhaustive studies in an attempt to identify the primary positive agent or agents of this original, non-traumatic phlebitis. Thank you, ladies and gentlemen.

I left the podium immediately and returned to Nixon's room. Ziegler continued the news conference, answering reporters' questions. I checked to see if my orders had been fully implemented. I approached Nixon's bedside and asked him how he felt.

"Jack," he said, "I'm miserable—if I ever get out of this

hospital, I'll never enter one again." "Dick, remember, I feel certain we can conquer this problem. Give me more time," I replied. Nixon responded, "I've respected your judgment and counsel for the past twenty-five years. I'll give you the time you want." Nixon then dozed off into a restless sleep.

4

The Plot Thickens

THE NEXT MORNING I REVIEWED a transcript of Ziegler's portion of the news conference. As I read Ziegler's responses, I became aware that he was often attempting to answer complex medical questions without adequate knowledge. I was upset that reporters were taking advantage of him in this situation and creating a circuslike atmosphere that was distorting Nixon's true medical condition and my decisions as his personal physician. Ziegler was conscientious in his replies, but I could see that some reporters were already raising the specter of mental dysfunction, psychiatric illness, and a cover-up "plot." One reporter even suggested that Nixon was wearing "pancake makeup" when he arrived at the hospital. (This was untrue—Nixon's complexion was pale and sallow because of his physical condition.)

The allegation of a "plot" arose when a reporter questioned the timing of my daily medical bulletins, which were to be issued at 3:00 P.M. The reporter complained that the timing would not permit them to make the network television news programs. The reporter asked Ziegler, "If the doctor examines him in the morning and is ready by 11:00 P.M. to tell us what is the matter with him, couldn't it be moved up? It seems like some kind of a plot." Ziegler's response was terse and direct. "Things never change," he replied. "The more they change, the more they stay the same." Explaining that he had meant 3:00 P.M. eastern time, Ziegler said the bulletins would be issued at 12:00 noon Pacific time.

Later that morning I encountered Ziegler in a hospital hallway, and this gave me the opportunity to share my thoughts: "Ron, I am concerned about the abusive tempo of the questioning, which I know you are used to. I realize that many of the questions have a medical component which you are not familiar with. I think that this puts you in an unfair position and allows the press to distort the true story. Therefore, I want to personally conduct all major press conferences in the future." Ziegler agreed with me and left the press conferences in my hands.

That afternoon we began our routine testing, including a chest film, which was normal, and a perfusion lung scan, which revealed a possible small embolus or blood clot in the right lung. This was followed by an airway-passage scan that confirmed the existence of a blood clot in the right lung. Upon receipt of these results, I immediately informed Nixon of this additional complication. "Well, Jack," Nixon said, "this is just another problem, and we'll have to deal with it. I hate to be lying here with this thing in my vein for many more days." I told him that I felt it necessary to conduct a news conference the next morning on the blood clot. Nixon agreed.

I called a news conference early in the morning on Wednesday, September 25, and informed the assembled press corps that Nixon had a clot that had moved from his leg into the lung. I added that this was potentially dangerous but not critical. I reminded the press that, despite this grave complication, the former president had "a helluva will to live." I concluded by saying that should a serious risk of another clot be imminent, I might order surgery to tie off a major vein and prevent such a catastrophic event. During the next few days, Nixon's condition remained stable, and the treatment proceeded satisfactorily.

On September 26, I received a telegram from Texarkana, Texas. A medical colleague of Dr. Michael DeBakey, the world-famous heart surgeon, admonished me with unsolicited medical counsel and offered to send Dr. DeBakey to California to assist me: "I have requested Dr. DeBakey to go to California. Please advise me Friday." I did not follow up.

On September 30, a week after admission, I went to Nixon's room and informed him that I had received a request from the press for a news conference about his medical condition, diagnostic study, and treatment. The request had come in the form of a letter from Roy Neal of NBC News, who suggested that a general news conference be held with the questions coming from a panel of selected reporters. Neal had proposed this to avoid the circuslike atmosphere of the earlier conference and to provide an opportunity for a more detailed analysis of the former president's condition.

"Doc, go to it!" Nixon said, "Give them hell! You can handle the vultures." I left Nixon and went to the first-floor conference room where the press was waiting. The room was filled with reporters and news cameras. I stepped up to the podium and began my remarks:

Good afternoon. Just a few off-the-record remarks if I may. This particular exercise was not suggested by me. This was requested by representatives of the news media. I had nothing to do with the selection of these individuals. Incidentally, I got permission from the former president and he told me "OK. Give them hell!"

From my own standpoint, I'm a bit confused. From some of you I get the impression I'm doing a good job, but others are more skeptical. Such statements as the rumor that this is a hoax is a despicable remark as far as I'm concerned. Anybody knowing me or my background knows that this is impossible. I've been in the practice of medicine for thirty years, and I resent certain innuendos and will leave it there.

"Is that comment off the record, Doctor?" a reporter asked. I repeated that it was off the record.

"Who suggested that there was a hoax?" queried another.

"I've seen it in the news reports, yes. I've heard it and that, please gentleman, is entirely off the record," I replied.

Before I took another question, I introduced the pool reporters selected by the media themselves. They included Roy Neal (NBC News), Larry Altman (*New York Times*), Stephen Greer (ABC News), Rick Davis (CBS News), George Getz (*Los Angeles Times*), Lee Markeles (Associated Press), Jack Fox (UPI), and Ben Zinser (*Long Beach Independent Press Telegram.*) I then reemphasized the high standard of medical ethics that I was bound as a physician to observe: "I again must strongly suggest to you that all my remarks that I give to you are again couched in what I respect, highly respect—the confidentiality of doctor and patient relation."

The next question was charged with politics. Rick Davis of CBS News asked if I foresaw any possibility in the next few weeks, even in the next few months, that Mr. Nixon might be able to travel to Washington to testify at a trial. My response was direct: "Now you're getting political, politically oriented. I don't want to be that way—I want to give you my professional opinion." Davis replied he was asking "purely on a medical basis." I explained that there would be a normal course of convalescence, which would be "restricted"; that particular course, however, had not yet been determined. I did not have all the test reports back at that time and would not until the beginning of the following week. I concluded: "I think that's about as far as I can go at this time, gentlemen." More questions followed; some were medical in nature, while others dealt with politics and with Nixon's psychological state.

The issue of Nixon testifying at the Watergate trial arose again. A reporter asked, "Doctor, from what you said today, isn't it highly unlikely that Mr. Nixon will be able to make a personal appearance in Washington during the duration of the trial?"

"I have no idea in the first place of how long the trial is going to last and I don't think anybody else does," I answered.

"Assuming—," the reporter started.

Cutting him off, I said, "Well, I am not answering assumed questions."

The reporters were relentless in questioning me about my veracity and the possibility of a "hoax." A reporter asked whether any physicians had been appointed by the U.S. District Court holding over the Watergate trial to verify my diagnosis. This question, of course, anticipated the court-appointed panel of physicians that would travel to San Clemente to examine Nixon, which I will discuss in a subsequent chapter.

Another reporter again raised the issue of a hoax. "Some people around this country wonder if Mr. Nixon really has to be in the hospital. Would you have any comment on that?" he asked.

I refused to dignify the question with an answer.

Considering the tenor of the questions, I felt that we needed a humorous perspective. Lee Markeles of the Associated Press had referred to my description of the size of the clot in Nixon's lung as about the size of dime. I said the problem probably was that Nixon had swallowed an FDR dime! (Actually, Nixon was an admirer of Franklin Delano Roosevelt's leadership qualities.) Unfortunately, few reporters laughed.

Nixon continued to improve in the days following the press conference. Further tests ruled out any malignancy as the primary cause of the phlebitis. During the week, Nixon's condition stabilized. I told him that if the remaining tests were negative, I would discharge him on Friday, October 4. The tests were negative, and Nixon left the hospital on Friday. At a news conference following Nixon's discharge, I told the news media that his convalescence would continue for one to three months.

One week later, I drove to San Clemente for a follow-up examination. When I arrived at La Casa Pacifica, I was met by Chief Robert Dunn, Nixon's U.S. Navy medical corpsman. We entered the grounds in a golf cart with my medical bag and briefcase. Chief Dunn told me that the atmosphere was much more relaxed because of the departure of several Secret Service agents. The House Appropriations Committee had cut transition funds for Nixon by more than half, from $850,000 to $398,000. I believed that this was imprudent. There was a vindictive atmosphere pervading the nation, which was reflected in the hate mail and threatening letters I had received.

I was receiving hate mail from as far away as Australia. I received a letter suggesting that I give Nixon cyanide and take it myself. Letters came from Oyster Bay, New York, Darien, Connecticut, and Woolloomooloo, Australia, calling me the "lowest moral example of a doctor," a "venal pigmy," a "disgrace to the AMA," a "criminal collaborator," "propagandist," and "cesspool dweller." The letter from Australia conferred on me an honorary degree: "Dr. John C. Lungren, Q.K. (quack)." I even received letters attacking me personally from members of my own profession. One such letter was from a distinguished cardiologist, an associate professor of medicine at a prominent eastern university teaching hospital, who wrote me: "Everyone recognizes that Nixon is a notorious liar. But are you so gutless that you also can't speak the truth."

A critic from the Washington with a Ph.D. censured me as well: "I'm surprised at you! As a longtime friend of RMN, you should have known that the anticoagulants wouldn't work on your bloodless 'patient.' Look at your x-rays again, and you will find that the clots are either icicles or clumps of bitter bile."

However, I also received many expressions of support. A professor of pharmacology and friend at the University of North Carolina, wrote, "Congratulations! Everything I've read or heard . . . clearly shows how superbly you have handled a very difficult assignment."

My wife received a heartfelt letter from my friend, the Reverend Jerome J. Wilson, C.S.C., vice president for business affairs at the University of Notre Dame. At this time, not only was I receiving hate mail, but the media was distorting my care of Nixon in television, newspaper, and magazine reports. Father Wilson's letter lifted my spirits:

> Rest assured, one of my real comforts is that a
> man like Doctor John is treating President Nixon.
> I feel the man needs the best treatment he can
> get. I know Doctor John has only the highest
> medical ethics in anything he does or says about

the former President's health. While I cannot condone the things Mr. Nixon did in connection with Watergate, I shall always be grateful to him for taking some of the fear and hatred out of our lives in making contact with China and Russia and for settling the Vietnam War. I, for one, did not want us just to walk out of Vietnam. . . . History is giving the two of you a chance to play a significant part, so take courage, for the good Lord gives you the strength each day.

Dunn and I found Nixon relaxed in a chaise lounge, fully dressed by the pool. He was wearing a heavy support-stocking on his left leg. I asked him how he felt. He said that he was beginning to regain his strength and was following my instructions to the letter. I told him that in two weeks we would need a follow-up lung scan. (Twice a week, Corpsman Dunn sent me a sample of Nixon's blood to determine the proper anticoagulation dosage.) Nixon said he hoped that this would not entail overnight hospitalization. I assured him that an overnight stay would not be necessary. As I left, I told Nixon I was spending the weekend in Pauma Valley where there was a fine golf course. "God," Nixon said, "how I wish I could play golf again."

My wife and I left for Pauma Valley. Pauma is a beautiful valley north of San Diego settled by the Luiseno and Pauma Indians and lying below the great observatory on Mount Palomar.

On Sunday morning, October 13, I was playing golf on the Pauma Valley Country Club course, when the club manager drove up in a golf cart and interrupted the game: "Dr. Lungren, President Nixon is calling you. I'll drive you back to the clubhouse, where you may talk privately in my office on the hotline."

"Hotline?" I exclaimed.

"Yes, we have a hotline just like President Nixon had when he was in the White House," he said proudly. (In 1963, a direct teletype link was set up between the United States and the Soviet Union on a special phone called the "hotline" on which President Nixon could send a teletype message to Brezhnev. It was not red but black and white).

I picked up the phone, and Nixon's voice greeted me on the hotline. "Jack, Pat and I would be delighted to have you and Lorain join us for dinner this evening at Casa Pacifica. Can you make it?"

"Dick, we would be pleased and honored, especially since I am able to respond on the hotline," I answered, explaining about the manager's hotline phone.

"Fine," he laughed, "see you about six."

We arrived at La Casa Pacifica at 6:15 P.M. delayed by heavy traffic. The Nixons greeted us warmly. Because we were delayed, the Nixons said they had worried that we had been in an accident. Nixon was dressed in a suit and Pat was wearing a soft, yellow-colored knit dress. I noticed that Pat had lost significant weight and that her face appeared taut, revealing to me that the cumulative stress of Watergate had taken its toll.

They escorted us out to the swimming pool, where we had a magnificent view of the Pacific Ocean. We returned to the living room to enjoy a cocktail before dinner. At dinner, the early conversation was confined to an informal discussion of our families.

Both Nixons appeared relaxed but somewhat troubled. As the conversation progressed, the Watergate trial took center stage. Suddenly, Nixon looked at my wife and me and said with impassioned consternation: "Pat and I would both like to know—*what did we do wrong?* I've always known that since the Hiss Case, I have been one of the most controversial politicians in Washington, constantly opposed by the liberal press," Nixon continued, "but why the double standard?"

"How well I remember the media's bias; in fact, I'm beginning to feel it now myself," I interjected.

Pat Nixon said vehemently, "I would have destroyed the tapes, but Dick's legal honesty prevailed—we can't destroy evidence."

Nixon looked at me and declared with evident anguish and remorse over what he had allowed to happen in Watergate: "My excesses were never greater than any of my predecessors. Yet I attempted to protect my closest friends and in the process let my country down." Driving home later, I reflected with sadness on how often loyalty is blind and how none of us—no matter how high or low—is immune from the consequences of his or her own fallibility. Nixon's tormented query—"what did we do wrong?"—revealed his surprise at his own guilt. Nixon would come to understand the theme John Milton explores in *Paradise Lost*: As human beings, we are all surprised by sin.

God left the will free to obey his law, explains Milton, as when the will obeys the moral law mirrored by "right Reason." The will is free because reason reflects the moral law and such obedience is freely given. Yet reason must be vigilant of the free will transgressing the law, "Lest by some fair appearing good surpris'd / She dictate false."[1] Tragically, in the case of Watergate, the dictation was false. The writing of the disaster then commenced.

Nixon's growing self-awareness would later deepen into dreadful self-recognition that would a reach a catharsis of conscience during the seminal David Frost interviews of March 1977. As he confronted his own actions, the consequences flowing from his own fallibility would fill Nixon with great sorrow and deep contrition. Nixon lamented that he had gravely harmed democracy in America by estranging a generation of young people from politics and by losing the chance for a generation of peace.

5

On the Campaign Trail
I

I SHARED NIXON'S ANGUISH OVER lost opportunities because I witnessed during the 1950s his potential for great leadership. In 1952, I joined the Nixon campaign in Washington, D.C., in mid-October to cover the final three weeks as campaign physician. I was entering the world of politics, a colorful, vibrant, kaleidoscopic world filled with a cast of characters who could just as likely be found in a novel by Charles Dickens. There were aspiring true believers and self-appointed confidantes, hangers-on, rogues and sycophants, potentates and genuine paladins. It was also a special universe where committed men and women sacrificed privacy and economic gain and summoned the best in themselves for the nation's common purpose.

There were characters like "Ditto Boland" in Edwin O'Connor's great novel of Boston politics, *The Last Hurrah*. Boland was the prototypical "hanger-on," imitating his political patron in every word, gesture, mannerism, and article of clothing. Hence, the name "Ditto." As the ever-servile adjunct to his patron's ego, Ditto offered uncritical praise in almost any context and for any occasion. Such undifferentiated flattery would become familiar to me, as I would hear it constantly offered to Nixon on the campaign trail.

The 1952 election campaign had its own distinct pace and rhythm. America had emerged from World War II as the guarantor of peace. Dwight D. Eisenhower, the great war hero, was running against an articulate, intellectual midwestern governor, Adlai E. Stevenson of Illinois. President Truman had decided not to run to avoid being discredited by scandals in his administration. Americans were fighting a fierce war in Korea. The American economy was expanding as the World War II generation began raising families, building homes, and buying cars.

Jack Drown and I had discussed the need for strong political leadership when we met at dinner parties with our spouses. Helene Drown and my wife, Lorain, had met in 1948 through their membership in the Junior League of Long Beach, working on volunteer community service. Born in Boston, Helene Drown had come west to be educated, and she earned a degree at UCLA. She began teaching and met Pat Nixon, then Thelma Ryan, who had studied at USC, while they were teaching high school in Whittier. They became best friends for life.

Helene Drown became a strong influence and friend to the Nixon daughters, Tricia and Julie, and a close confidante to Pat Nixon. Jack Drown became one of Richard Nixon's closest advisers and friends. They traveled often with the Nixons when Nixon was out of office; their daughter Maureen became a very close friend of the Nixon girls. Jack Drown's introduction of me to Nixon in 1952 made my four-decade friendship with him possible.

Jack Drown was born in Long Beach and earned an appointment to West Point, but he severely injured a knee playing football. Drown transferred to Stanford, continued playing football, graduated, and then enrolled at USC law school where he met the attractive, intelligent, and tenacious Helene Drown. A community activist, articulate and outspoken, Helene Drown cared deeply about the future of the United States as represented by its youth and the next generation. Although Jack had passed the California bar examination, he managed his aging father's magazine distributorship. A large man with a hearty, infectious laugh and an adroit, wide-ranging intelligence, Drown had keen insights into local and national politics as well as a knowledge of foreign-policy issues.

The "Dick Nixon Special" left Washington, D.C., early on a Monday morning in 1952 for a swing through the key eastern states of New Jersey, New York, Pennsylvania, Ohio, and Illinois. On the train, Jack Drown introduced me to Rose Mary Woods. I was immediately impressed by her forthright demeanor, quick intelligence, and friendly smile. Red-haired, pretty, and Irish-Catholic, Woods was the "fifth Nixon," an all-around "girl Friday" acting as Nixon's personal secretary, executive assistant, trouble-shooter, adviser, alter ego, and close confidante.

Born in Sebring, Ohio, Woods had come to Washington in 1943 and had met Nixon while working as a secretary for the Herter Select House Foreign Affairs Committee dealing with the reconstruction of Europe after World War II. Robert Sam Anson described Woods well: "Her duties had little to do with stenography or typing. Rose Woods more often took names than dictation. She knew who the friends were and who were the enemies, who had helped— often and when—and who hadn't, who was owed, and who wasn't. She was the gatekeeper, guardian and mother protector, and her loyalty was fierce and absolute."[1]

Wood's closeness to Nixon was perceived as significant, not only by Washington insiders but even by foreign gov-

ernments. For example, in Moscow in 1972, at a state dinner in Nixon's honor hosted by an ailing Soviet President
Leonid Brezhnev, Yuri Andropov, director of the KGB, who
was to become Brezhnev's successor, sat next to Woods.
During the dinner, Andropov turned to Woods and asked
her, "Madame, would you like to share a bottle of wine with
me, the finest wine in the Kremlin?"

Woods knew that something was not right. Andropov's
offer was an audacious breach of diplomatic and state protocol. As Brezhnev's subordinate, Andropov was upstaging
the Soviet president, the evening's host. Intrigued and wary,
Woods decided to play along and said yes. Andropov summoned a waiter and made the request. The wine was delivered to Woods and Andropov as Brezhnev commenced a
toast to Nixon. Woods knew what Andropov was up to—he
was sending a tacit signal to Nixon that he was in charge of
the Soviet Union—not Brezhnev.

Woods and I developed a close friendship, and during
the campaigns, schedule permitting, we would go to daily
Mass together. During the Watergate ordeal, Woods confided a fearful experience: her apparent responsibility for
the famous recording gap in one of the Nixon tapes crucial to Watergate. She was interrogated by law enforcement
and congressional authorities about her now-renowned
"Rose Mary stretch." Woods explained that in reaching from
her desk to her credenza, she inadvertently erased the tape
for eighteen-and-a-half minutes.

Woods found herself at the center of an international
firestorm; in a photograph of her demonstrating the
"stretch," she appeared on the front pages of magazines
and newspapers around the world. Woods was in need of
loving and trusting friends, as indicated by her letter to
Lorain and me:

January 14, 1974
Dear Lorain and Jack:
    The recent situation which confronted me
was, as you can imagine, a frightening and
embarrassing one. The wonderful words of
encouragement and understanding which I
have received from dear friends like you were
more helpful to me than you will ever know,
and I just want to tell you how grateful I am
for your thoughtful message.
    With kindest personal regards and best
wishes for the New Year.

Sincerely,
Rose Mary Woods
Executive Assistant to the President

    In 1952, there was only one other person who had such
an intimate professional and confidential relationship with
Nixon as did Rose Mary Woods—Murray Chotiner. A hard-
driving, portly, cuff-link-wearing, cigar-smoking Los Angeles lawyer with a sallow complexion and quick wit, he loved
politics and hated his bail-bonds law practice in Beverly Hills.
    Chotiner was a brilliant, abrasive, and passionate po-
litical strategist whose campaign instincts were so acute and
effective that his opponents feared him as the "Machiavelli
of California politics."[2] He had grown up under rather
tough circumstances, as Roger Morris explained: "Chotiner
was the son of a cigar maker in Pittsburgh who had mi-
grated to the [Los Angeles] basin to run a chain of movie
theaters and soon abandoned the family with some cruelty,
leaving Murray and a brother to support an embittered,
difficult mother. After a year as an undergraduate, he had
gone to the Southwestern College of Law in Los Angeles,

THE WHITE HOUSE
WASHINGTON

January 14, 1974

Dear Lorain and Jack:

The recent situation which confronted
me was, as you can imagine, a frightening and embarrassing one. The wonderful
words of encouragement and understanding
which I have received from dear friends
like you were more helpful to me than
you will ever know, and I just want to
tell you how grateful I am for your very
thoughtful message.

With kindest personal regards and best
wishes for the New Year,

Sincerely, *Love,*

Rose Mary Woods
Executive Assistant
to the President

Dr. and Mrs. John C. Lungren
2898 Linden Avenue
Long Beach, California   90806

*Sorry not to have had a chance
to see you in California!*

and finished at twenty, the youngest graduate in the school's history."[3]

Chotiner believed that you either play politics to win or get out of the game. One morning during the campaign, Chotiner, Drown, and I went out to a coffee shop for breakfast. Chotiner outlined his strategy for winning: "First, a basic truth—you *must define* your opponent, *never* let the opponent define you. If he does, you're through, pure and simple," he declared. "Then you find your opponent's weakness in his record and conduct—he's too liberal, he's soft on defense, he's easy on criminals, he's got ethical and character problems—and you move in, hitting harder and harder—with no letup," he said. "And you never give voters more than they can handle. They have their own lives. Most people can't absorb more than two or three issues during a campaign. So limit your themes, focus and refine the issues, and drive them home again and again," Chotiner concluded.

As the campaign progressed, I began to learn a little more about Nixon. I noticed that he was a person of extraordinary discipline who could work tirelessly twelve to eighteen hours a day. Nixon also had the ability to express himself with clarity and force to his advisers. In addition, it became evident to me early in the campaign that Nixon could not handle criticism easily. I had the feeling that he was more comfortable when surrounded with people who agreed with him.

Nixon's relationship with William P. Rogers, a young confidante on the trains, illustrates this point. Rogers was a lawyer whom Nixon had first met during the Hiss case, when Rogers was counsel on a Senate subcommittee investigating allegations of government espionage. A protégé of Governor Thomas Dewey, Rogers was a district attorney from New York. He had earned Nixon's confidence in August of 1948, during the investigation of allegations of espionage against State Department official Alger Hiss by Whittaker Chambers, a former communist and editor at *Time* magazine. Rogers read transcripts of Chambers's testimony before the House Un-American Activities Committee, and he was impressed with it. Rogers encouraged Nixon to pursue Chambers's evidence against Hiss, who was later convicted of perjury.

Handsome and vain, highly intelligent and ingratiating, Rogers often provided Nixon with valuable political advice. On September 22, during the 1952 campaign, Nixon conferred with Rogers on the night before the "Checkers" speech, trying out various themes as they walked the streets behind the Ambassador Hotel in Los Angeles and swam in the hotel pool. Nixon appointed Rogers as secretary of state in 1969.

I found Rogers personable and likable; however, he frequently offered gratuitous praise instead of candor and constructive criticism. Unfortunately, Rogers was a yes-man and would tell Nixon that he was great and that everything was fine when it was not. Rogers personified a disturbing pattern in Nixon that I perceived as he rose to greater positions of power: a predilection to surround himself with advisers who were completely subservient.

At times, loyal and trusted advisers who were not afraid to tell Nixon when he was wrong were shunted aside. These usually were advisers who were personally and intellectually secure, who wanted and needed nothing from Nixon. Their forthright counsel was allowed to wane in favor of influence from those who feared jeopardizing their own acquired power and position.

A few weeks later, when our train reached New York, we campaigned in the southern part of the state. In those days, we would travel during the week, hitting campaign stop after campaign stop. We would spend the weekend in a large city or resort area reviewing the previous week and planning strategy for the next. At the end of my first week, the campaign team stayed at the Plaza Hotel in New York for the weekend.

Jack Drown and I were in our hotel room at the Plaza on Friday evening, relaxing and discussing the week's events. It was midnight, and I heard a knock on the door. I opened it and a woman was standing there with two bags of luggage. It was my wife, Lorain, who had flown in from California as a surprise. Jack Drown, Helene Drown, and Lorain had a wonderful weekend enjoying New York. It was an exhilarating time when the World War II generation had come of age and was entering its prime, and we felt that these changes were mirrored by America. Yet, the modern political campaign was in its infancy in 1952. Air travel had not yet supplanted the campaign train, but it would soon do so. The Santa Fe "Dick Nixon Special" was one of the last trains used for about half of the itinerary in an American presidential campaign. The year 1952 still reflected an earlier era in which conversations were kept private. The tape recorder was too cumbersome for personal use; good writing was a prerequisite, and reporters still used the heavy but indispensable Underwood typewriters. Personal computers—not yet dreamed of in 1952— would never have the same idiosyncratic feel as a reporter's Underwood keys. Nor would words recorded on tape emerge as resonant and true, as I would discover twenty-two years later, when Watergate predominated the headlines.

Jack Drown, who bore the title "Train and Plane Manager," had published a small yellow-and-blue-colored booklet titled *Service Guide for the Dick Nixon National Campaign Tour*. This campaign guide had a section titled "Typewriters," which explained that because of the "rapid campaign schedule from train and plane to hotel or rally," transportation for typewriters would not be provided. Therefore, reporters should keep them in their own possession. It also noted that the campaign would fly on a DC-6B aircraft, which would carry extra typewriters available on a large table in the rear of the plane. The section immediately following "Typewriters" was titled "Western Union." This section noted that the Western Union representative, Mr. L.B. "Larry" Rawls, would assist reporters in making their deadlines. Rawls and his staff would be on duty "day and night whether aboard the train, plane, at the hotel or auditorium." The campaign booklet explained: "Larry Rawls has alerted all Western Union offices along our entire route. Even where we do not stop, Western Union representatives will be at these depots to make pickups as Larry pitches them off in special bags." The booklet further pledged to reporters that "every effort will be made to have your stories on the wire within minutes after they have been filed." Stories written by today's reporters are transmitted around the world not in canvas mailbags but in software-driven "real time" amounting to milliseconds—virtually instantaneous— yet, as I would discover, they often lack the reflection, clarity, and perception of the earlier stories.

By the middle of October, Nixon was drawing crowds larger than Eisenhower or Stevenson. Major newspapers began assigning their top reporters to the Nixon campaign. In September, reporters traveling on the "Dick Nixon Special" from Pomona to Seattle were primarily from California and Oregon. There was national press represented, but it included only the *New York Times, Time* magazine, Copley Press, and United Press International. By October, however, the national press was clamoring to travel with Nixon. Reporters covering the Nixon campaign included most of the national press: *Christian Science Monitor, New York Herald Tribune, Washington Post, Chicago Tribune, St. Louis Post-Dispatch,*

Detroit News, Omaha World Herald, De Moines Register, Newsweek, and the *U.S. News & World Report,* as well as reporters from the Associated Press, *Meet the Press* (NBC), and the Mutual Broadcasting System. The national press assigned their best reporters, and they wrote lead stories, sensing Nixon would make good copy for the kind of dramatic narrative for which they were famous. Among these reporters were Bill Lawrence, James Reston, and Arthur Krock (*New York Times*); Bert Andrews, Joseph Alsop (*New York Herald Tribune*); Roscoe Drummond (*Christian Science Monitor*); Walter Trohan (*Chicago Tribune*); James Shepley, Hank Luce (*Time-Life*); Ernest K. Lindley (*Newsweek*); Clark Mollenhof (*Des Moines Register*); May Craig (*Portland* [Maine] *Press Herald*); and Martha Roundtree (*Meet the Press* [*NBC*]). There were also two reporters who later became famous novelists, Fletcher Knebel (*Seven Days in May*) and Allen Drury (*Advise and Consent*).

Many of these men and women were reporters' reporters, men and women who devoted their lives to the honored craft of journalism. They lived for narrating great events, cared deeply for the written word, and had a sense of history's deep currents and dramatic political, social, moral, and spiritual rhythms. The experience of World War II made these reporters acutely sensitive to history and the politics of leadership. They knew that the most dangerous time for any generation is when there is a political vacuum. Reporters of this era had witnessed the devastating effect of World War II—a whole generation of potentially great leaders lost. Hitler filled the resulting void with brigands, gangsters, thugs, and his own malevolence. They knew that elections are often definitive expressions of a generation's awareness of its responsibilities and destiny. Nixon became acutely aware of such vicissitudes of politics during the 1954 campaign.

The election campaign of 1954 was Nixon's first as vice president and one in which he was virtually responsible for the entire Republican slate of congressional and gubernatorial candidates across the country. During this campaign, I learned more about Nixon's deep concerns about his public image and the effect it had on his family.

I was not planning to be involved in Nixon's 1954 campaign because I had received a postgraduate fellowship in cardiology from the National Heart Institute and was taking a year off from my medical practice to study with Dr. George Griffith at the USC School of Medicine. I was already three weeks into the fellowship program when I received a call from Jack Drown in early October: "Jack, the 'Boss' is in poor health both mentally and physically. He wants you to join the campaign for a week and treat what is ailing him." I replied that I would, and I requested permission from Dr. Griffith, who granted me a two-week leave of absence. I flew to Corvallis, Oregon, to meet the vice president's campaign. I gave Nixon an immediate physical examination and determined that he had a flu virus and laryngitis. I prescribed appropriate medication, and he responded well. I stayed with the campaign for nearly two weeks as it whistle-stopped its way east to Denver.

This was a grueling campaign for Nixon. He was troubled by the increasing personal attacks on him by the Democrats, including Adlai Stevenson, who was positioning himself to run again for president in 1956. Eisenhower was of little help; trying to stay above congressional and gubernatorial politics, he had relinquished responsibility for campaigning on behalf of Republican candidates and handed the job to Nixon. In the 1954 campaign, Nixon flew 26,000 miles, visited 95 cities in 31 states, and campaigned for 186 House, Senate, and gubernatorial candidates, delivering 204 speeches and holding more than 100 press conferences. During the campaign, the *New York Times* assigned five reporters, including Cabell Phillips and Peter Kihss, and a photographer, George Tames, to cover Nixon. (Tames later became famous for his silhouette portrait of President Kennedy bending over reading newspapers in the Oval Office.)

The sharp personal attacks of Stevenson and the Democrats were taking their toll. Eisenhower's decision to stay above the fray left Nixon as the Democrats' primary target. Cabell Phillips described Nixon's role in the *New York Times:* "[Nixon] is not only the chief strategist of the campaign now being waged across the country, he is the main assault force."[4] "Jack, I'm beaten both physically and mentally," Nixon confided to me in Corvallis. "Maybe this should be my last campaign. I'm becoming the chief bad guy of American politics. I know that Pat doesn't like the set up and the girls are reaching an age where they are sensitive to the attacks on their father," Nixon complained. This was the first time that I had seen Nixon lack the "fire in the belly" for his political career. Nixon cared deeply for his family. Pat Nixon was his best friend and confidante. Nixon's love and concern for his daughters, Tricia and Julie, was strong. Nixon's doubts about his political future, as expressed to me in 1954, revealed a man only too aware of the potential travail and anguish his political future could cause him and his family.

After the election, on November 19, Nixon wrote me: "This is just a note to tell you how much I deeply appreciated your joining our campaign trip from Corvallis to Denver. Apparently your advice and medication was exactly what I needed because everybody has remarked since I returned to Washington that they have never seen me looking better! I know what an inconvenience it was for you to take off as you did from your work and for that reason I particularly appreciated your going along with us."

The Republicans did better than expected in the 1954 election, losing twenty seats in the House of Representatives and two seats in the Senate—far less than had been predicted. Nixon's campaigning had prevented the anticipated Democratic sweep, and Republicans from grassroots precinct walkers to President Eisenhower were grateful. On November 15, 1954, *Newsweek* assessed Nixon's contributions: "Nixon was the sparkplug of the entire Republican campaign. Early in the year, when the Republicans were smug and somnolent, waiting for peace, prosperity, and the Eisenhower name to give them victory, it was Nixon who kicked them awake."[5]

The presence of two key members of Nixon's staff made the 1956 campaign particularly rewarding and interesting. They would become pivotal figures for Nixon in his career. Though they came from different backgrounds, newspaper editor Herb Klein and lawyer Robert Finch were close friends. Each had an intuitive grasp of politics and advised Nixon with candor, perspective, and foresight.

Herb Klein was a slim, sandy-haired former reporter who had risen rapidly from copy boy to editor at the *San Diego Union*. Desiring first to become a sportswriter, Klein had become sports editor at Roosevelt High School and at the University of Southern California. As a reporter for the *Alhambra Post-Advocate*, Klein had covered the debates between Nixon and Congressman Jerry Voorhis in Nixon's successful 1946 campaign. Klein was a political independent who had voted for Franklin D. Roosevelt. However, he felt an affinity for Nixon since both had served in the Navy; reporting on Nixon stimulated Klein to take a major interest in postwar politics and government.[6]

Klein's easygoing, affable exterior belied his courage in standing tall on principle and in giving Nixon negative news and constructive criticism. As a reporter and editor, he had earned the respect of his peers with his crisp writing style, fair and accurate reporting, and editorial balance. Hugh Sidey of *Time* magazine once wrote of Klein: "His journalistic bearings never faltered."[7] Acting as Nixon's assistant press secretary in 1956, Klein attempted to establish rapport between Nixon and reporters, mediating between them, opening Nixon up, and disabusing reporters of misperceptions. Often Klein would confront Nixon and tell him that he had to open up or suffer continuing misapprehensions by the press. "Typically, the idea that there was a new Nixon," Klein observed, "seemed to crop up at the start of each campaign and to disappear about midway." Klein explained that Nixon would allow himself to become more accessible to the press early in the campaign and then withdraw from the press, feeling he was being mistreated.[8]

Klein's closest friend on the Nixon campaign staff was Robert Finch, a young, astute former marine and California lawyer who was Nixon's alter ego and "political philosopher."[9] Handsome and engaging, Finch at age thirty-one was a politician with a love of ideas and a passion for justice. Finch had first met Nixon in 1946 in Washington when Finch was an assistant to Congressman Norris Poulsen (later mayor of Los Angeles). Nixon's congressional office was down the corridor from Poulsen's. Nixon and Finch would meet often, discussing foreign policy and civil liberties. Finch convinced Nixon to vote for the Marshall Plan to aid in the recovery of postwar Europe. Nixon counseled Finch to return to California to attend law school.

Born in Tempe, Arizona, Finch was the son of a war hero and cotton farmer who had been elected as a Republican to the Democrat-controlled Arizona legislature. The family moved to Inglewood, California, when the cotton farm failed. Even after becoming a school-supply salesman to support the family, Finch's father never let him forget the vocation of politics—to serve something larger than oneself. Finch was determined to prepare himself for such service. A star high school football player and editor of the school newspaper, Finch excelled as a leader. He was elected class president in high school, at Occidental College, and at USC law school. As a student at Occidental, he won a national college speech competition with a compelling address on Andrew Jackson.

Finch ran unsuccessfully for Congress in 1952 and 1954. He became chairman of the Los Angeles County Republican Central Committee from 1956 to 1958, where he gained more knowledge about political strategy and organization. Finch ran Nixon's 1960 presidential campaign against John F. Kennedy. In 1966, Finch ran for lieutenant governor of California and won, receiving ninety thousand more votes than Ronald Reagan, who won the governorship. Finch would become so close to Nixon that in 1968 Nixon offered Finch the vice presidency. He declined because he believed that Nixon needed a running mate from a state other than California. When Nixon was elected president, he offered Finch the position of attorney general, which he declined in favor of becoming secretary of Health, Education and Welfare. This Cabinet position turned out to be a bureaucratic morass, ill-suited to Finch's political idealism. Finch resigned within two years to become counselor to the president, where his influence was curtailed by already entrenched powers in the White House.

Finch's travails revealed a troubling characteristic of Nixon and the political world in general that I could neither fathom nor condone—the tendency to discard loyal aides when they become dispensable. The pattern was familiar—the aide would never be informed directly, overtly ostracized, or summarily dismissed. He was merely ignored, cut out of key meetings, gradually stripped of responsibility, given a position with no authority, and, in effect, shoved into a corner. Herb Klein was also placed in political exile. Both Klein and Finch kept their dignity, but they never recovered their influence and effectiveness. Nixon suffered unnecessary political defeats without their constructive counsel and mature and balanced perspective.

Of course, the fates of Klein and Finch were yet to unfold. Both were valuable assets in the campaign of 1956. In October of that year, I joined the Nixon campaign in Detroit where we were to begin a tour through the Michigan peninsula. Since we were not far from South Bend, Indiana, I suggested to Nixon that a visit to Notre Dame, my alma mater, for a rally would be beneficial and would also allow him to see the university's beautiful campus. Nixon admired Notre Dame's football accomplishments as models of excellence, superior teamwork, and discipline inspired by brilliant, charismatic coaches—in particular, Knute Rockne, Frank Leahy, and later, in the 1960s and 1970s, Ara Parseghian.

The Notre Dame students gave Vice President Nixon a warm, enthusiastic welcome. The highlight of the day was Nixon's visit to Cartier Field, the revered practice field where Knute Rockne had coached the Four Horseman and other Notre Dame football legends. As we watched the Notre Dame team practice, I realized that Pat Nixon had achieved something unprecedented—she was the first woman to set foot on the field.

In 1956, Nixon knew that Eisenhower had little desire to run for reelection. Rumors about Eisenhower's lukewarm view of running again reached the press and were published in the newspapers. Various Republican factions began to believe that the presidency was up for grabs. In California, a group organized a committee for Earl Warren, the former

California governor whom Eisenhower had appointed chief justice of the United States. In the midwest, supporters of Ohio Senator Robert Taft began to organize as well.

Nixon realized the Republican Party was in a weakened position. He was concerned that the party would divide itself and forfeit the presidency. This scenario stirred Nixon's competitive instincts, and he decided to fight hard to retain the vice presidency. At the same time, an aggressive "Dump Nixon" campaign was being waged by Nixon's rivals in the party. In an off-hand comment, Eisenhower himself even suggested that Nixon consider taking a Cabinet position. As the "Dump Nixon" movement continued into the fall of 1955, Nixon's rivals in the administration also campaigned against him. Then an unforeseen event intervened, dramatically altering the political landscape. On September 24, 1955, President Eisenhower suffered a heart attack, and Nixon was thrust into the consciousness of the American public in a way he had never been before.

"I had to provide leadership without seeming to lead," Nixon recalled, describing the difficult situation in which Eisenhower's heart attack had placed him. Nixon performed this delicate role very well, with a business-as-usual demeanor—resolute, firmly in command, yet never suggesting that he was usurping presidential powers. Nixon's conduct caused Eisenhower to place greater confidence in him, and this eventually led to his renomination as the vice-presidential candidate at the Republican Convention in San Francisco in August. Nixon's father, Frank Nixon, died on September 4 after rupturing an abdominal artery—an event that, as Ralph de Toledano described, "put the first real lines of age on his face."[10]

In 1956, I was assigned the last three weeks of the campaign, joining the chartered and well-equipped United DC-6B *Nixon Special* in Detroit. The plane was large enough to carry the vice president, his staff, and twenty-five journalists. Many of the reporters assigned to cover Nixon in 1956 were openly adversarial. The most antagonistic was Phil Potter of the *Baltimore Sun.* Ralph de Toledano described Potter as openly declaring his bias and announcing to his colleagues what he intended to do to Nixon: "[Potter] frankly stated his dislike of Nixon and swore that he would make him lose his temper before the campaign was over."[10] Fortunately, most reporters covering Nixon had more self-restraint than Potter and conducted themselves professionally or at least camouflaged their bias more deftly.

6

On the Campaign Trail II

THE YEAR 1960 WAS A WATERSHED in American political history. Two young men, whose lives were shaped by World War II and had entered Congress together in 1946, ran against each other for the presidency. The lives and careers of Richard Nixon and John F. Kennedy would intertwine often but never so much as during the election of 1960. The campaign was the most dramatic, the most issue-oriented, the most intense, and the closest in modern American politics. Nixon and Kennedy mesmerized the nation.

In 1960, I was to cover the last three weeks of the campaign. When I joined the campaign in mid-October, three issues dominated conversation among the press and staff—the debates with Kennedy, Kennedy's health, and the Catholic issue. These subjects were discussed around the clock in hotels and on planes and trains.

In 1960, when the campaign was in Oakland, California, Nixon asked to see me in his hotel suite. I went to his room and found Nixon alone. "Jack, there is something I want to discuss with you in confidence. It's about Kennedy's health," Nixon began. "I have heard that JFK is suffering from a chronic disease. What is Addison's disease? Does this condition affect his mental functions in any manner?"

"Dick, according to reliable reports Kennedy does have Addison's disease," I answered. "Do you recall that Kennedy was plagued by an old back injury which he received during the war? The fact is that I believe in the fall of 1954 you visited him in the hospital when he had a recurrence and needed surgery. Kennedy then suffered adrenal failure due to complications from the operation," I continued. I began explaining to Nixon the pathology of Addison's disease, a condition in which the functions of the adrenal gland won't produce hormones in sufficient quantities. The adrenal gland slows production or becomes completely nonfunctioning, and the patient suffers from fatigue, weight loss, and an irritable stomach.

I mentioned to Nixon, "Perhaps you know, there have been rumors that India Edwards, co-chairwoman of Citizens for Johnson, had told reporters in July that if it were not for cortisone Senator Kennedy would not be alive." With Addison's disease, the administration of cortisone is absolutely necessary for survival. If cortisone is used for a long period of time, the patient's skin becomes bronze and when exposed to the sun develops a healthy tan. When you give cortisone injections, the gland gradually ceases normal function and no hormones are produced. The patient must take cortisone the rest of his life.

In concluding my discussion of the disease, I informed Nixon that "all systems of the body can function inadequately, including mental faculties." Nixon was quiet for a moment. He finally declared, "Jack, this is a personal subject and we will not use it in this campaign."

In 1954, Dr. James A. Nicholas, a New York City orthopedist, performed a lumbosacral and sacroiliac fusion on

Kennedy. Dr. Nicholas claims that the original diagnosis of Addison's disease was made by physicians at the Lahey Clinic in Boston. This diagnosis was confirmed by the late Dr. Ephraim Fhorr, who was the professor of endocrinology at Cornell University School of Medicine. An optimistic evaluation of Kennedy's disease was expressed by his physician, Dr. Janet Travell. She stated that he had a history of thirteen years on steroid maintenance with no evident modifications of mood. His drug treatment was completely managed by Dr. Eugene Coken, a Cornell endocrinologist, all through his presidency with frequent evaluations of his physical condition.[1]

Nixon's decision not to use Kennedy's health as a campaign issue revealed to me a sense of fair play and personal honor that was also manifested in Nixon's decision not to contest Kennedy's victory in 1960 despite strong evidence that voting fraud may well have deprived Nixon of the office. Nixon believed that a contested election would do great harm to the nation by damaging confidence in its institutions.

In 1960, the response of Kennedy's campaign regarding his Addison's disease was vague and varied. Dr. Janet Travell actually denied that he was taking cortisone. "Senator Kennedy does not take cortisone. But he does take a relative of cortisone. These are natural constituents of the body," Travell announced at a news conference. Kennedy himself was seriously concerned about disclosure of his Addison's disease and how it would negatively affect his public image. In the December 1, 1997, issue of the *New Yorker*, Gore Vidal, who was once related to Kennedy through his stepfather's marriage, described a frenzied phone call from a very worried Kennedy. In the spring of 1959, according to Vidal, Kennedy called him regarding an article to be published in *Esquire* magazine. Vidal recounted that

Kennedy said: "That friend of yours up there, Dick Rovere. He's writing a piece for *Esquire* about 'Kennedy's last chance to be President' or something. Well, it's not true. Get to him. Tell him I don't have Addison's disease. If I did, how could I keep up the schedule I do?"[2] Rovere never made the disclosure in the *Esquire* article. Vidal worried about this self-censorship as well as his own failure to report what he knew about Kennedy's Addison's disease: "I can see that, subliminally at least, my knowledge of his [Kennedy's] Addison's disease was bothering me then, just as not having gone public with it in 1959 bothers me now."[3] Public disclosure of the health of a president or presidential candidate is crucial for the American political system to function with integrity.

Theodore H. White covered the Kennedy and Nixon campaigns in 1960; his reporting established a new genre in political journalism—the campaign chronicle. White's book *The Making of the President, 1960* won the Pulitzer prize, and he made a career of covering presidential elections with his fast-paced, dramatic narratives. White was a distinguished reporter and journalist who had attended the Boston Latin School and graduated summa cum laude from Harvard University in 1938. He reported in China as a *Time* magazine correspondent and then as chief of *Time*'s China Bureau. Returning to the United States, he edited General Joseph Stilwell's papers and then became European correspondent for *The Reporter*.[4]

"Teddy" White was the darling of journalism in the 1950s and 1960s. He was a war reporter who parlayed his skills into fame and celebrity, much as Edward R. Murrow had done after covering World War II from London. White's career anticipated the age of the independent journalist, self-conscious of a cultivated omniscience, usually unaffiliated or standing apart from a newspaper, writing books that are awaited eagerly by the general public. David Halberstam, Seymour Hersh, Carl Bernstein, Bob Woodward, and J. Anthony Lukas are the best-known practitioners of this genre. I vividly remember the arrival of White aboard the Dick Nixon Special. We were whistle-stopping through the upper tier of midwestern states. Jack Drown and I were standing on the steps of the reporters' Pullman car during a station stop. Suddenly White jumped on the steps. He had just left the Kennedy campaign and had come over to our campaign to see how it was progressing. White was wearing a large "Kennedy for President" button on his overcoat lapel.

"Glad to see you, Mr. White. Welcome aboard," Drown exclaimed.

"Why the decoration?" I asked.

"I'm going with the winner," White replied with some belligerence.

In contrast to this prediction, White wrote in *The Making of the President, 1960*: "The last ten days of the 1960 campaign produced a surge for Nixon. Had the campaign gone on two days longer and had Nixon been physically capable of maintaining the pace he might well have forged into the lead. As it was, he had reduced Kennedy's lead in the polls to zero."[5]

Despite his evident bias, I believe White's reporting was for the most part balanced and fair. The *Making of the President* series achieved bestseller status, a testament to White's journalistic skills in his dramatic narratives of American politics.

On February 23, 1960, Notre Dame's senior class awarded Nixon the university's Patriotism Award. The annual award was presented on Washington's Birthday to an American whose achievements reflected the wider sense of community obligation and sacrifice. The Patriot of the Year was expected to use the occasion to deliver a speech about American values and the national purpose. The Patriotism Award grew out of Notre Dame's Washington Birthday Exercises, a university tradition since 1849.

Previous recipients included FBI Director J. Edgar Hoover, Bishop Fulton J. Sheen, General Curtis E. LeMay, Senator John F. Kennedy, Robert F. Kennedy, and Wernher von Braun. The mixture of liberal and conservative recipients reflects the tenor of the times, the divisive and polar tension in American political life during the Cold War, which would erupt in the 1960s and 1970s in the national crises of civil rights, Vietnam, and Watergate. This tension continued after Nixon's award in 1960, as seen in three succeeding Patriotism Award honorees: Admiral Hyman Rickover (1961), Bob Hope (1962)—a welcome respite from the tension—and Adlai Stevenson (1963).

Senior Class president Richard Corbett read Nixon's award citation to the packed audience in the University Drill Hall. The language was florid yet to the point:

> We praise you as a courageous and energetic
> interpreter of the American idea to the world.
> With patient zeal—and on occasion heroically
> facing hostility—you have gone out among the
> nations to win new respect for all that we mean as
> a people.
> You also share and effectuate, we believe,
> Washington's conviction that if this land is pre-
> served in peace and tranquility it can bid defiance
> in a just cause to any power whatsoever. And at
> this annual celebration we honor you, Sir, not
> only as a preserver of our national power and of
> the justice of our national cause but especially as a
> preserver of the peace of America and the world.

The language of the citation reflects an era when patriotism was viewed as a virtue essential to the national purpose. American values were a binding force that radiated through society from citizens to the republic. Nixon's Patriotism Award speech and Adlai Stevenson's speech three years later were serious, eloquent meditations on the ultimate destiny of the American republic. Unfortunately, the fragmentation of political discourse, the lack of serious thought, and the rhetorical emptiness of our politicians have frequently failed the test of leadership. Nixon and Stevenson's Notre Dame speeches, however, mirrored the shared intellectual patrimony and rhetorical heritage from St. Augustine to Edmund Burke and Thomas Jefferson, Abraham Lincoln and Woodrow Wilson to Pope John XXIII.

Nixon, who was introduced by the president of Notre Dame, the Reverend Theodore M. Hesburgh C.S.C., importuned the students to a similar patriotic dedication: "When you go out from this University, may I urge you . . . to strike at ignorance, strike at provincialism, strike at prejudice wherever it rears its head. . . . May I use just one example with which your president, Father Hesburgh, has had such a distinguished career—the issue of civil rights. Here is an opportunity for you, who have had a chance to attend this great University, to help in leading the fights in your communities and in this country against prejudice and for the realization of equality of opportunity for all our people."

The condition of candidates' health was a significant issue in 1960. Soon after the Republican convention in Chicago, during a campaign stop in Greensboro, South Carolina, Nixon banged his knee on a car door. The wound developed into a severe hemolytic staphylococcus infection and high fever by the end of August, and Nixon was hospitalized until September 9. Afterward, he lost weight and appeared pale and sallow.

Nixon and Kennedy went into the first debate on September 26 with Nixon ahead, but the debate concluded with Kennedy gaining the lead by a small margin. Kennedy had turned the election to an even match due to better preparation and a far better projected image for the television audience. In his memoir, *Tell Me a Story,* producer Don Hewitt notes that Kennedy seemed to take the debate very seriously, while Nixon viewed it as another campaign event. Kennedy changed his campaign schedule a week before to meet with Hewitt in a Chicago airport hangar and receive briefing on the logistics of the debate. On the afternoon of the debate, Kennedy rested in his hotel room. Hewitt recalls that Nixon did not take such precautions: "On the day of the debate, instead of resting up and saving his energy that was already sapped by a staphylococcus infection, Nixon met with the Plumber's Union—not realizing that the meeting was peanuts compared with what he had committed himself to do that evening."[6]

Hewitt had flown one of the best makeup artists, Frances Arvold, to Chicago for either candidate to use. Kennedy used her only briefly. Nixon declined the offer and instead used his own makeup specialist, Ted Rogers, who perplexingly applied a cosmetic product called "shavestick," which accentuated Nixon's heavy beard and sallow complexion under the intense lighting of the studio.

The second debate was held in Washington on October 7, eleven days later. Nixon knew he had to fight the negative image of a weakened and emaciated candidate that was projected during the first debate. He drank four milkshakes a day to put on much-needed weight, and he also decided to let Frances Arvold do his makeup.

Nixon went on the offensive, criticizing Kennedy for a

statement made in May of 1960. The Soviet Union had shot down an American U2 spy plane piloted by Frances Gary Powers, and Kennedy felt that Eisenhower should apologize to Krushchev. Nixon argued that "an American president should never apologize for actions taken to defend America's security."[7]

The third debate between Nixon and Kennedy was held on October 13 in Los Angeles, where I had just joined the campaign for the final three weeks. I had been briefed by my campaign-physician colleagues, Dr. Malcolm Todd and Dr. Hubert Pritchard, on Nixon's health, including the two-week admission at Bethesda Naval Hospital because of the knee infection that had developed before the first debate. Both doctors felt that this infection had diminished Nixon's effectiveness during the campaign and the first debate. However, they believed that Nixon had made a complete recovery and was mentally and physically as sharp as ever.

I went to Nixon's suite to assess his condition for myself, and he greeted me warmly: "Jack, glad to have you on board again. How is the family?" He went on to assert, "Todd and Pritchard have me in good shape again. I'm going to continue on the offensive."

"Dick, my family is very well, thanks. I received a positive report from Mac and Hugh. Do you need anything?" I asked.

"No, Jack," Nixon replied, "I'm ready for this third debate and for the Al Smith Dinner in New York on the 19th. I will be seeing you after the performance tonight." Nixon "performed" well in the third debate. Christopher Matthews described the third debate as "the Republican candidate's strongest performance."[8]

On October 19, we were in New York at the Waldorf-Astoria for the fifteenth annual Alfred E. Smith Memorial Foundation Dinner. The event was named in honor of the first Catholic to run for president, Al Smith, former governor of New York. The dinner raised money for Catholic charities in the New York Archdiocese and was sponsored by the archbishop, who in 1960 was Francis Cardinal Spellman. Over the years, the affair had become one of the great rituals of American politics, a "must" event for any presidential candidate. Those invited were a political "who's who" in New York and national politics. In 1960, the guests included New York Governor Nelson Rockefeller, Mayor Robert Wagner, U.S. Senator Jacob Javits, and *Time* magazine founder Henry Luce.

The archbishop had invited candidates Nixon and Kennedy to address the dinner. Nixon accepted immediately. Kennedy vacillated because of his concern over being identified too closely with the Catholic Church, thereby alienating non-Catholic voters. In his memoirs, however, Nixon stated that Kennedy's Catholicism, while perceived as a liability, was actually an advantage: "The pockets of fundamentalist anti-Catholic prejudice that still existed were concentrated in states that I stood to win anyway. But many Catholics would vote for Kennedy because he was Catholic, and some non-Catholics would vote for him just to prove they were not bigoted."[9]

It should be noted that many of Nixon's confidantes and members of his staff were Catholic, including Rose Mary Woods, Daniel Patrick Moynihan, and myself. I can recall Nixon's interest in Catholicism. Nixon was sympathetic to government funding of parochial schools, believing that the inculcation of moral and religious values was essential to the national interest. Also, Nixon was attracted to Catholicism itself, once telling Charles Colson that he "could be comfortable being a Catholic."[10] Nixon expressed similar thoughts to me on more than one occasion. William Safire related a conversation on Catholicism between Nixon and Daniel Patrick Moynihan: "Pat, you're Catholic aren't you?" Moynihan nodded yes. "You believe in the whole thing?" The tone of the question was respectful, but Moynihan was never the reverent type. "Not only that Mr. President," he replied, cocking his head at H.R. Haldeman and John Ehrlichman—both Christian Scientists—"I even believe in doctors."[11]

By late October 1960, Nixon's campaign continued at full throttle. The campaign was attempting to visit all fifty states. The schedule was as intense and demanding as any campaign itinerary imaginable, with quick turnarounds and flights through often-difficult weather. The media and the candidate were already in an uneasy relationship; each needed the other to get their recompense beyond surviving the rigorous travel schedule together. Add to this the stormy weather and the close quarters of airplanes, and animosities—personal and otherwise—were set to erupt.

In Cheyenne, Wyoming, our large chartered jet attempted to land during a driving snowstorm. We circled the airport for a long time. The governor of Wyoming ordered snow-removal equipment to prepare the runway for landing. Once the snow was removed, the pilot made three passes, and on the fourth approach we landed safely. During the flight, several reporters had panicked and begun blaming their imminent demise on Nixon's desire to visit all fifty states. The most disturbed of the reporters was NBC's Sander Vanocur, an articulate journalist with immense self-possession, who lost control and screamed, "The vice president's obsession is going to get us all killed!" The attendants heard Vanocur's outburst and reported it to the pilot.

After Nixon's speech at a local high school, we returned to the plane. I saw several reporters gathered around the front landing wheels, chanting and yelling at Vanocur, who was on the tarmac: "Hey Sandy, check the landing gear! Is it safe to take off?" After a smooth takeoff, the pilot turned on the cabin intercom and announced: "My name is Captain Block. I'm a senior pilot for American Airlines. I have flown jets for six years. The landing and take-off follows strict FAA procedures. Incidentally, I live in Palos Verdes, California, and have a wife and eight children. I'm just as anxious to arrive home safely as you are."

The 1962 campaign did not require my presence on a daily basis. My participation in Nixon's unsuccessful California gubernatorial campaign against incumbent Pat Brown in 1962 was minimal. Since the campaign was confined to California and I was available for consultation at any time, a team of physicians was not needed.

My wife Lorain was more involved. She organized "A Nixon Day in Long Beach" in which Nixon appeared at coffee receptions and teas scheduled every ninety minutes during the day and, finally, at a dinner in the evening; the event raised $16,500, a considerable sum in 1962. She even enlisted my medical colleagues as volunteer drivers for Nixon and his campaign staff.

Haldeman, who was running the 1962 campaign, was impressed, and he asked Lorain if she would travel throughout the state and present tutorials on how to organize "A Day with Richard Nixon." Haldeman, who was known even then as "Mr. Super Advance," told her it was the most successful day of fund-raising he had ever seen. Lorain declined because she was totally involved with raising our seven children. She did, however, write a "how to" report which was distributed to the Republican Party throughout the state.

Nixon's decision to run for governor was one of the worst in his long political career. The decision was made after he had been summoned to the White House by President Kennedy to discuss the Bay of Pigs disaster. Naturally,

Nixon's political juices began flowing again, and he decided to run for governor against his better political judgment. Nixon knew that it would be difficult to defeat the popular Governor Pat Brown, a California-bred, Irish-Catholic politician whose political vision was reshaping California's future with massive infrastructure investments in the California Water Project and the University of California system. In addition, the Kennedy White House was pouring money and assistance into the race to defeat Nixon and cut short his political rivalry with JFK.

One rivalry that would not be cut short was the famous Notre Dame–Army football series, which had been renewed in the 1960s. On the night of October 9, 1968, when Lorain and I were in New York City, we attended a Notre Dame–Army game at Shea Stadium with Dick and Pat. The Irish won 17-0. This was only a few years after Nixon's double defeat for the presidency against John F. Kennedy and for the governorship of California against Pat Brown. Before the game, during halftime, and at the final whistle, Nixon was mobbed by the great crowd wanting to talk with him and obtain his autograph. I noticed that the public's fascination with Nixon never seemed to diminish throughout his entire career, whether he was in or out of office. The intense response of the crowd was an echo of the nation's pulse and revealed that Nixon's career was far from over.

7

The Haldeman Enigma

WHITE HOUSE CHIEF OF STAFF H.R. Haldeman stood as the last of a long line of ambitious Nixon aides who achieved power by ingratiating themselves and gaining un-adulterated favor with him. Once ensconced in a position of power, they maintained their privilege and influence by curtailing access of other Nixon staff or *anyone* they perceived as a rival.

A devout Christian Scientist, Haldeman was an ambitious perfectionist who ingratiated himself to Nixon with aggressive efficiency: "every president needs a son of a bitch, and I'm Nixon's. I'm his buffer and his bastard."[1] Haldeman even harshened his handsome features by wearing a Prussian-style brushcut. His aggressive efficiency had a self-aggrandizing aspect that was harmful because it often left Nixon without the free give-and-take of opinions and ideas that accompany good decision making.

Haldeman had worked in the Nixon campaigns as an advance man under Robert Finch in 1956, 1958, and 1960. Born into a prominent Southern California commercial family that had made money in a Pontiac car dealership, Haldeman graduated from UCLA in management and marketing. Haldeman rose quickly at J. Walter Thompson, a famous advertising agency, to become a senior executive.[2]

Bob Haldeman was always an enigma to me. I could never fathom why someone with such a successful career in public relations and advertising for a company as prestigious and productive as J. Walter Thompson would feel his position threatened by supposed rivals. Moreover, Haldeman had a wonderful, loving wife and family who stood beside him in times of crisis. Perhaps he just did not understand doctors—his religion discouraged the use of medical science. Sadly, Haldeman waited too long to contact doctors after it was discovered that he was suffering from cancer, and he died in 1993.

As a student at UCLA, Haldeman was impressed by Nixon's intellect. Haldeman waited outside the Hollywood theater where Nixon gave the Checkers speech in 1952 to present a letter volunteering his services to the campaign. Although this initial offer to volunteer was not accepted, Haldeman was able to join the 1956 campaign through a UCLA classmate, Loie Gaunt, a dedicated Nixon secretary and staff assistant. Haldeman, although only an advance man in 1956, would later acquire immense influence and power with Nixon. Julie Nixon Eisenhower assessed the consequences of Haldeman's behavior: "Haldeman was a very negative person who didn't want anyone close to my father."[3] Haldeman once kept philanthropist and ambassador to Great Britain Walter Annenberg waiting for half an hour while he sat in his office telling jokes to an aide. Although a genuinely affable and generous man, Annenberg never forgot the insult and refused to contribute to Haldeman's Watergate defense fund.[4]

I found that the best way to deal with Haldeman was to confront the problem immediately, as I would during the 1968 presidential campaign. I joined the 1968 campaign in New York City. It was mid-October, and I was to cover the final three weeks of the campaign. The staff had chartered three Boeing 727 passenger jets, one called *Tricia* for the candidate and staff, one named *Julie* for the writing press, and a third plane for radio and television reporters. Reporters would be assigned to Nixon's plane on a rotating "pool" basis that changed every day. Haldeman, who was the day-to-day campaign manager, assigned me to the press plane *Julie*, to hotel rooms as far away as possible from Nixon's suite, and to the press bus at the tail end of all vehicles in the motorcade. This was intolerable for a campaign physician.

Nixon, of course, knew nothing about what was happening regarding Haldeman's assignments and assumed that everything was fine. In previous campaigns, I had been assigned to Nixon's plane, to a hotel room on the same floor as his, and to a car in the motorcade next to his limousine. I could not fulfill my duties under these circumstances. I decided I would resign and leave the campaign if Haldeman's orders were not contravened. I went to the Secret Service and had a frank discussion with Secret Service agent Rex Scouten, who later became chief of the White House ushers. "Rex, Haldeman's actions are unacceptable for Nixon's safety and security," I began. "How can I, as Nixon's physician, treat the candidate if I am assigned to a different airplane, on a bus at the rear of the motorcade, or at the most distant room from Nixon in the hotel? Rex, I won't be able to remain on the campaign under these circumstances."

I had to say no more. Scouten said he would address the problem. Following this discussion, I found myself assigned to Nixon's plane, to a hotel room close to him, and in the Secret Service convertible directly behind the candidate in the motorcade. This arrangement never changed for the rest of the campaign.

Haldeman also tried to banish Rose Mary Woods, but he was only partially successful. While Haldeman could move her office away from the president's or keep her out of meetings, he could not erase the implicit bond of trust and loyalty between Nixon and the red-haired Irish-Catholic from Sebring, Ohio, whose keen intelligence and political savvy had caught the attention of the Kremlin and Yuri Andropov.

In early October 1970, I called Rose Mary Woods at the White House and asked her to check Nixon's calendar for 1971 to determine his availability to address the twentieth annual plenary session of the American College of Cardiology. The following week Woods phoned and informed me that Nixon had accepted and would be delighted to address the plenary session. I began working with the American College of Cardiology and its executive director, William Nelligan. We determined with the White House that Nixon would speak to the cardiologists on the morning of February 4, 1971, in the ballroom of the Sheraton Park Hotel in Washington, D.C. The American College of Cardiology would present Nixon with its highest honor: the ACC Freedom Medal.

On February 3, my wife and I arrived in the early afternoon at Dulles International Airport. We were transported to the Sheraton Park Hotel by limousine. Upon arrival, I immediately called Rose Mary Woods to reconfirm my appointment with the president at 3:00 P.M. in the Oval Office to discuss his speech and the expectations of the international audience of distinguished cardiologists. I arrived at the White House fifteen minutes early. At precisely 3:00 P.M., I was admitted to the Oval Office by a Secret Service agent. The president was at his desk with his usual yellow legal pad in front of him.

"Hello, Jack, I am really glad to see you. How are Lorain and all the children?" Nixon asked. I said they were fine.

"I asked you over this afternoon, of course, to review tomorrow's activities with the American College of Cardiology," Nixon continued. "Tell me about the American College, its organization, members, and history." I explained that the American College of Cardiology had been founded twenty-five years earlier and that its members consisted of cardiologists from all fifty states and many foreign countries. "Given the present national concern over health care, this is a significant meeting and speech to a group of highly trained professionals in cardiology, a field that has seen the greatest advancement in medicine during the past fifteen years," I said. Nixon listened intently. "Mr. President, give them leadership in the development of a health delivery system," I concluded. Our discussion had lasted forty minutes.

I returned to the Sheraton Park Hotel. The next morning at 7:00 I was awakened by a phone call from one of Haldeman's staff assistants at the White House. He informed me that the president must cancel his appearance and speech at the plenary session and that we should present the ACC Freedom Medal to Nixon at the White House later in the day.

I was stunned. I hung up the phone and exclaimed to my wife, "My God, I have to call Rose immediately!" Upon reaching Rose Mary Woods, I explained that Haldeman had canceled the president's speech. I had to say no more.

"Jack, hold everything, I will be back to you as quickly as possible," she instructed.

Within ten minutes, Rose called me back.

"The morning session is scheduled as originally planned. The president will be there on time," she stated.

Obviously, despite widely circulated speculation about Haldeman's domination of the White House power structure, there was still one formidable person with whom he had to contend—Rose Mary Woods, the "Fifth Nixon."

At 9:00 A.M. Nixon arrived at the Sheraton Park, where he was received by a packed ballroom of cardiologists. A wave of thunderous applause arose as he entered. Nixon's speech was well received. He stressed the need to retain the fee-for-service health-care delivery system. In his speech, Nixon acknowledged the great ongoing national debate over health care, which continues to this day. The president called for "better methods to see that all individuals who need medical care have an opportunity to obtain it." He expressed his concern that the debate over the quantity and delivery of health care should not be allowed to affect the quality of health care and the autonomy of the physician. "Let us do everything we can to keep the doctor, the professional man or the professional woman, free from the terrible crushing burden of bureaucracy, which would otherwise not only take his time, but destroy his initiative," Nixon declared. Following the speech, Dr. William Sodeman, president of the American College of Cardiology, presented Nixon with the Freedom Medal. The president left to a standing ovation.

Haldeman also attempted to interfere with the plans of my daughter Loretta, who was then a student at St. Mary's College in Notre Dame, Indiana. In the spring of 1971, Loretta had been awarded a White House Summer Internship. She was going to work for the White House Office of Communications, where she was assigned to help prepare the president's daily briefing, marked "For the President's Eyes Only." In late May, Loretta had come home to California to prepare for her move to Washington for the summer. However, the day before Loretta was to leave to begin the internship, she received a phone call from one of Haldeman's White House secretaries, who informed her that her internship was cancelled—no explanation was given. Loretta was devastated and began sobbing. Struggling to compose herself and regain her self-possession, Loretta called me at my office and told me what had happened. I said I would call Rose Mary Woods to find out why.

When I reached her, Rose said, "Jack, don't worry, I'll do some background and find out what has happened." Forty-five minutes later Rose called back and said, "Loretta will be a White House Summer Intern for President Nixon."

Rose had gone directly to the president: "Mr. President, there seems to be some confusion regarding the White House interns. Have plans changed? Haldeman's office called Jack Lungren's daughter Loretta in California and told her that her internship was cancelled."

"There are no changes," the president replied. "I anticipate Loretta and all other designated interns are to begin as scheduled. Welcome Loretta personally for me and say that I am pleased she will be here."

Haldeman could not curb his often-perplexing conduct even at Pat Nixon's funeral in 1993, years later. After the funeral, Nixon received former staff and close friends in the foyer of the Nixon Library. Stanchions were set in the foyer to guide the mourners to where Nixon was standing at the head of the reception line.

Former White House chief of staff Alexander Haig and communications director Herb Klein stood waiting in the long line with their spouses along the stanchions. Haldeman and his wife simply ignored the receiving line altogether. They stepped over the stanchions in front of everyone to shake hands with Nixon and engage him in an extended conversation while everyone else waited. Former Nixon staff members who were waiting in line to offer their condolences to Nixon were baffled at Haldeman's brazen and inexplicable breach of receiving-line protocol. Sadly, Bob Haldeman always remained an engima.

8

Defeating Death

DURING THE FALL OF 1974, in the days when Nixon had invited Lorain and me to dinner and expressed his feelings of remorse over Watergate, I consulted with him by telephone at regular intervals about his recovery. It was during this period that I received a phone call from Nixon's lawyer, Herbert J. Miller, regarding the Watergate trial. He told me that William H. Jeffress Jr., one of his associates, would be calling me to take an affidavit for my signature on the state of Nixon's health and physical condition.

Jeffress called me on October 2. I swore an affidavit to be presented to Judge Sirica. My considered medical opinion was that Nixon's phlebitis was life-threatening and unless he had adequate time for appropriate therapy and recovery there was a serious risk of further clotting and hemorrhaging. My medical consultants on Nixon's case, Siebert Pearson, Eldon Hickman, and Earl Dore, concurred with my diagnosis.

Miller also sent me the proceedings of the U.S. District Court for the District of Columbia, *United States of America v. John N. Mitchell and defendants.* In the trial, Watergate chief prosecutor James Neal insinuated that I was stonewalling and protecting Nixon from testifying. Miller vigorously challenged this assertion: "One thing I would like to call to the Court's attention. The Government in its opposition, and I am sure unintentionally, in a way seemed to question the integrity, although they said they were not, of Doctor Lungren, and I want the Court to know in addition to Doctor Lungren there were three other doctors who examined Mr. Nixon. They have had no prior relationship with him, went over all the tapes and the hospital record and the scan of the lung and they concurred, so I know that Doctor Lungren felt quite badly at the way the matter came out in the press. I think it was really unfair."

Judge Sirica replied: "I am sorry that happened."

Prosecutor Neal responded: "Your Honor, may I say one thing? First, there was no intention I am sure, and I speak for all the lawyers on my staff, to impugn any integrity of Doctor Lungren. We did point out that Doctor Lungren did not really address the issue of whether he could come and testify or not. He said he couldn't do certain things, but we simply pointed out those certain things could be avoided even though he came here." Neal was attempting to practice medicine as a lawyer, always a difficult balancing act.

On October 23, late in the afternoon, Nixon came to Long Beach Memorial Hospital for the scheduled lung scan and venograms of his lower legs. The lung scan revealed no evidence of new clots. However, tests showed that the anticoagulation medication was inadequate. This inadequacy of oral anticoagulation was a concern and reached the point where I believed that he was suffering a "paradoxical effect," the inability to properly anticoagulate with oral medication.

The venogram of Nixon's left leg revealed blood-vessel blockage in the femoral vein of the upper thigh. While the venogram of the right leg was entirely normal, the blockage in the left leg presented a danger of further clots advancing to the lung and causing a fatal massive embolism. I decided to hospitalize Nixon immediately to use intravenous Heparin again to thin his blood and try to reestablish an oral anticoagulation regimen. If this treatment did not work, I planned to order surgical intervention to prevent incipient clots from advancing to the lung.

On the following morning, I decided that we should hold a consultation of vascular surgeons. I called my colleague Dr. Eldon Hickman, a highly skilled vascular surgeon on the staff of Memorial Hospital and an associate professor of surgery at the UCLA School of Medicine. Dr. Hickman examined Nixon and concurred with my recommendation for continued anticoagulation therapy. However, because of Nixon's poor response to the therapy, Dr. Hickman and I sought another opinion. Dr. Hickman called Dr. Wiley Barker, professor of surgery at UCLA and an acknowledged expert in the field. Dr. Barker agreed to come to Long Beach for consultation. Dr. Barker recommended a radioactive blood-sampling test to determine whether Nixon's clotting activity was adequate or whether surgery was warranted.

On Monday night, October 29, Dr. Hickman and I decided that surgery was necessary. We scheduled the surgery for early morning Tuesday and informed Nixon. Upon hearing my decision, Nixon said, "Jack, I am glad you're here. Let's go and get it over with." I phoned La Casa Pacifica and spoke to Pat Nixon, and I also called Julie Eisenhower in Washington and Tricia Nixon Cox in New York City. I explained the necessity of the surgery, its risk, and my prognosis. The family responded with concern and hope for a complete recovery.

I informed the news media of the impending surgery, explaining both the reason and the risks involved. My statement read: "X-ray pictures made during the special test confirmed the presence of a large clot extending to the left external iliac artery, the vessel that connects the femoral artery in the thigh to the interior vena cava. Based on this concern, the doctors agreed that urgent surgery should be scheduled at 5:30 A.M. Tuesday." I also told the media that the operation involved exceptional risk because Nixon was taking blood-thinning drugs, which could loosen clots precipitously and fatally.

The clotting in Nixon's deep vein system in his left leg was so extensive that it blocked over 99 percent of the blood flow. If surgery were not performed to block the clot from traveling to Nixon's lung, the sure result would be death from a massive pulmonary embolus or lung clot. The approach I decided on was to insert what is known as a Miles clamp, essentially a small plastic filter or sieve which is placed around the occluded iliac vein just above the clot. The clamp pinches the vein to prevent the clot from flowing up the vein yet allows enough blood to flow to maintain the necessary circulation.

Nixon was taken to preoperation preparation at 5:00 A.M. We had scheduled the surgery early to accommodate Secret Service arrangements. When Nixon entered the surgical pavilion, the entire operating suite was locked. Secret Service agents were properly gowned and masked. Surgery began at 5:30 A.M. The surgical team consisted of vascular surgeons Dr. Eldon Hickman and Dr. James Patton, thoracic and cardiac surgeon Dr. James Harper, anesthesiologist Dr. Melvin Campbell, and myself.

Dr. Hickman placed the Miles clamp above the blocked vein after determining its location and size by feeling it and then isolating it with his hand. The operation was completed at 6:50 A.M., and Nixon was taken to a new, unoccupied intensive-care unit on the seventh floor of the hospital.

Nixon's postoperative recovery proceeded normally and uneventfully that morning.

I immediately went to the room where Pat Nixon was waiting. I told her, "Pat, I think Dick is sufficiently stabilized for you to see him." "Is he going to make it?" she asked. I replied, "I think so, but the next forty-eight hours will be the critical period." I then brought Pat Nixon into intensive care to see her husband. She was surprised at the paleness of his complexion and became worried. She called Tricia and Julie and asked them both to come as soon as possible. Rose Mary Woods had already flown out and was at the hospital with Pat Nixon.

I returned to my office to see my regularly scheduled patients. At 12:45 P.M. I received an urgent call from the hospital alerting me to problems with Nixon's blood pressure. When I arrived in his room, Drs. Hickman and Campbell were already there with a team of assistants and nurses. Nixon was alabaster-white, incoherent, and slipping into unconsciousness. His blood pressure fell dangerously low at 55/20, and his respiration was extremely rapid and frenetic. Nixon was in vascular shock. After the surgeons closed the surgical wound, Nixon's vital signs were in the normal range. However, in the recovery room, in spite of the outward signs of stability, a blood vessel began bleeding in the wound closure. Gradually, blood began to flow and accumulate in Nixon's inner abdomen.

The bleeding intensified, slowly at first, then more rapidly. The rupture became a massive flow of blood into the abdominal cavity and vital organs—heart, brain, kidney. In two hours, Nixon had plummeted into total shock; he would die within an hour if the vascular shock were not reversed. I ordered countershock measures immediately, including intravenous fluids, blood transfusions, shock positioning of the bed, and emergency blood work. Nixon received four units of blood—the vascular shock was caused by massive retroperitoneal intestinal bleeding.

Julie Eisenhower later described what had happened to her father: "while propped up on the edge of his bed, flanked by his navy corpsman, Bob Dunn, and a nurse, my father fainted suddenly and almost fell to the floor. Dunn and the nurse rolled him back on the bed, the nurse slapping his face several times, urgently repeating, 'Richard, wake up, Richard!'"[1] Our emergency measures stabilized his condition within three hours. Yet it was an extremely close encounter with death. Nixon had gone to the very edge of life, as he vividly described later:

> I remember the pinprick of the needle administered by the anesthetist and being wheeled down to the operating room, but for six days thereafter I was in and out of consciousness.
>
> My first recollection was of a nurse slapping my face and calling me. "Richard, wake up," she said. "Richard, wake up." I knew it was not Pat or Lungren. In fact, only my mother called me Richard. When I woke up again, Lungren was taking my pulse. I noticed I was hooked up to intravenous feeding and other contraptions. I told him I was anxious to go home. He said, "Listen, Dick, we almost lost you last night. You are not going to go home for quite a while!"
>
> When I woke up again, I asked Pat to come in. I now knew that I was in pretty desperate shape. Throughout the time we have known each other, Pat and I have seldom revealed our physical disabilities to each other. This time I couldn't help it. I said that I didn't think I was going to make it.

She gripped my hand and said almost fiercely,
"Dick, you can't talk that way. You have got to
make it. You must not give up." As she spoke, my
thoughts went back again to the Fund crisis in
1952. Just before we went on stage for the broadcast, when I was trying to get all of my thoughts
together for the most important speech of my
life, I told her, "I just don't think I can go through
with this one." She grasped me firmly by the hand
and said, "Of course you can." The words were
the same but now there was a difference. Then I
had something larger than myself to fight for.
Now it seemed that I had nothing left to fight for
except my own life.[2]

Nixon's condition stabilized and improved over the next
several days. On November 5, I learned that President Ford
was visiting California on a political campaign trip. My first
thought was that a visit by President Ford would be thera-
peutically beneficial to Nixon. I reached Admiral Lukash
at 7:30 that evening. Dr. Lukash was at the Century Plaza
Hotel in Los Angeles with President Ford's entourage. I
told him of Nixon's condition and said that a visit from
President Ford would be a great morale builder. On the
day of Ford's flight to California, White House press secretary Ron Nessen was saying that President Ford did not plan
to visit Nixon because of his critical condition.

Admiral Lukash then asked me about security at the
hospital. I told him that it was extremely good because
Nixon was the only patient on the entire seventh floor and
the Secret Service had secured it. Dr. Lukash said that he
would give my message to President Ford and asked that I
call him at 7:00 the next morning. I called Dr. Lukash
promptly at 7:00 A.M., informed him that Nixon continued

to improve, and again I recommended a visit from Ford. Lukash said the president planned to visit Nixon at 10:15 A.M. and stay approximately twenty minutes, part of the time with the family and the remainder with Nixon himself.

At 9:45 A.M., I met with the Secret Service to discuss arrangements for me to greet President Ford and escort him to see Nixon. I deliberately had not told Nixon of Ford's visit until a few minutes before his arrival so as not to overly excite him. After a meeting with the Secret Service, I went to the seventh floor to tell Nixon that President Ford was here to see him.

Memorial's new level had locking glass doors to private rooms, an innovative feature. I found the door to his room locked from the inside and was unable to enter. Hurried calls were made to the hospital maintenance department for a locksmith and carpenter. I was unable to tell Nixon of Ford's impending visit since the door was still not open, and I had to go quickly downstairs to welcome President Ford. I greeted President Ford as he stepped out of the limousine, exchanged pleasantries, thanked him for making the visit, and then escorted him to a waiting elevator in the main lobby. We walked through an applauding throng of people, including hospital staff, patients, the public, and the media.

On arriving at the intensive-care unit with President Ford, I found that the glass door to Nixon's room remained locked. I escorted the president into a nearby room where Pat Nixon, Tricia, Julie, and Rose Woods were waiting. President Ford kissed each one and spoke with them privately for five minutes. Meanwhile, I went to check on the glass door, which a carpenter had finally opened with a hacksaw. As I entered the room, Nixon made a humorous remark that was an obvious reference to the Watergate break-in:

"Jack, apparently they needed a safecracker to open the door." Nixon explained that he knew how to open the door but that I had told him not to get out of bed. It was then I told Nixon that Ford was there to see him. I escorted President Ford into the room.

It was a highly emotional encounter. Ford grasped Nixon's hand and whispered to him, "Be well." President Ford sat in a chair by Nixon's bedside. Ford asked if Nixon had had a good night. Nixon replied, "None of the nights are too good." They discussed international affairs and President Ford's planned foreign trips. After ten minutes, the president left the room, said goodbye to the Nixon family, and thanked the surgeons and me for our care of Nixon. President Ford was visibly moved by the visit and appeared subdued as he left the hospital.

The previous evening Monsignor Connolly, personal secretary to Cardinal Manning of Los Angeles, called me to express Manning's deep concern over Nixon's health. He said Cardinal Manning was offering special prayers for his recovery and would be available to visit Nixon if he so desired. I conveyed this to Nixon, who was most appreciative and said he would welcome a visit when he was feeling better. Nixon said with a twinkle in his eye, "Jack, what are you trying to do, make a Catholic out of me?"

"Dick," I replied, "I think that is an excellent idea."

Cardinal Manning did visit Nixon at a later date and they had a warm conversation. I saw Nixon later that same day after Manning had left the hospital. "Jack," Nixon said, holding up a cross, "now I really do think you are trying to convert me! Furthermore, I enjoyed the conversation with Cardinal Manning. But Jack, I want you to have this." He handed me the cross. I hesitated in taking it—but I did so at Nixon's continued insistence.

Nixon often discussed theological subjects with me, always emphasizing that belief in a Supreme Being was a primary prerequisite for peace. Also, Nixon stressed that such belief was essential for his own life and personal conduct. Nixon was not a man who wore his religious belief on his sleeve; he wore his faith in his heart.

9

Judge Sirica's Medical Panel

ON NOVEMBER 5, HERBERT MILLER, Nixon's lawyer, called me regarding Nixon's availability to testify under subpoena at the Watergate trial. On September 4, John Ehrlichman had issued a subpoena to Nixon to testify on all matters related "to the concealment or cover-up of the break-in" into the Democratic National Headquarters at the Watergate Hotel. I told Miller that Nixon would not be able to engage in any substantial mental or physical activity for two to three months and that it would be an indeterminate time before he had recovered sufficiently to travel long distances. Miller submitted an affidavit to this effect to Judge Sirica on November 7, 1974.

On November 13, Judge Sirica issued an order appointing three physicians to a panel to examine Nixon in San Clemente to verify my findings and prognosis. Judge Sirica charged the panel to advise the court of every conceivable situation under which Nixon could or could not testify:[1]

(1) whether Mr. Nixon is able now to travel to Washington and testify as a witness in this case;

(2) if not, when, in their opinion, Mr. Nixon would be able to so appear and testify;

(3) whether Mr. Nixon is able to appear and testify at a site near his home;

(4) if not, where, in their opinion, Mr. Nixon would be able to so appear and testify;

(5) whether, if Mr. Nixon is not now able to appear and testify in this case either in Washington or a site near his home, he is able to be deposed by the parties in this case;

(6) if Mr. Nixon is not physically able at the present time to give a deposition when, in their opinion, he would be able to give such a deposition;

(7) if Mr. Nixon is physically able to submit to a deposition, the conditions under which such deposition should be taken in order to avoid serious risk of injury to his health.

The signed judicial order also contained the signatures of the United States prosecutor James Neal and the defense attorneys for H.R. Haldeman, John Mitchell, and John Ehrlichman. The order contained the names of the three physicians appointed by Judge Sirica: Charles A. Hufnagel, Georgetown University; Richard Starr Ross, Johns Hopkins; and John A. Spittell Jr., Mayo Clinic. Sirica selected Hufnagel as panel chairman. Hufnagel was chairman of the department of cardiovascular surgery at Georgetown Medical School and was famous for his introduction of the first successful artificial heart valve, known as the "Hufnagel valve." Judge Sirica did not know that Hufnagel was a personal friend of mine and a classmate in the premedical program at the University of Notre Dame. Although he was a year ahead of me at Notre Dame, we shared close mutual friends and had maintained contact over the years.

I told Nixon of Sirica's decision to appoint a panel of independent medical examiners from the east. Irritated that a federal prosecutor was challenging my medical integrity, I ruefully suggested to Nixon that "maybe we should ask the American Bar Association to appoint three western federal judges to go to Washington and examine Judge Sirica." Nixon laughed and said, "Instead of three judges, the American Medical Association should send three psychiatrists to examine Sirica."

Nixon and Pat were extremely upset over the questioning of my medical judgment and integrity. They trusted me implicitly, and they knew that if I believed Nixon were physically and mentally capable of traveling to Washington to testify, I would have made that judgment without hesitation. Indeed, Nixon had told me that he would testify after a period of convalescence to regain his physical strength and mental energy. However, he also told me that if he were compelled to testify while he was hospitalized that he did not think that he could survive.

Nixon was very firm about the conditions under which he would be examined. He presented them to me almost as a legal brief: He would not submit to any tests or blood work the panel might suggest. His medical records could not be reviewed without a subpoena from the court or his written permission. His medical records could not be reviewed by any of the three members of the examining team without the presence of one of his physicians and a Secret Service agent at all times. His medical records were not to be removed from their secure position at Memorial Hospital. Any consultation fees resulting from requests by the panel to his physicians were to be submitted to Ehrlichman or Judge Sirica.

Nixon's concern for his privacy and his anger over Judge Sirica's appointed medical panel was such that he told me he would provide minimal cooperation. If the panel asked questions on how he felt, he would refer all questions to his physicians. Nixon also said that if the panel proved to be politically oriented, he would see to it that they were properly investigated for bias and prejudice. Nixon believed that I had been unfairly treated by the media.

Two serious medical issues arose as a result of discussions concerning the Sirica panel and their investigation of the integrity of my own medical judgment. The first was the regional rivalry between eastern and western medical establishments; the second was the professional division between practicing and university physicians, commonly called the town-gown dichotomy.

The Sirica panel was composed of eastern physicians, specialists affiliated with prestigious university hospitals at Georgetown, Johns Hopkins, and the Mayo Clinic. Although I was a specialist in cardiology and internal medicine and a clinical professor of medicine at UCLA, I was also a physician in private practice, affiliated with a regional medical center, Long Beach Memorial Hospital. These professional and regional conflicts manifested themselves acutely during this intense period when I was caring for Nixon and when his health was front-page news around the world. Some professors at Yale University Medical School and at Mount Sinai Hospital publicly criticized me for the choice of the vein on which the Miles clamp was placed to prevent the blood clots from traveling to Nixon's lungs.

Many of these irresponsible "interview-critiques" were given over network television, including the *CBS Morning News* and the NBC *Today* show. I remember watching one of these network programs and concluding that the physician expert's criticism was inaccurate, unclear, and unfounded. When asked about the criticism, I responded that I did not understand how physicians with no immediate knowledge of the case could be so critical if they were not familiar with the specific facts. Where I decided to have the clamp placed was the result of discussions with the surgical team and the highly regarded medical consultants at UCLA, including the university's chief of surgery and two prominent vascular surgeons. The Miles clamp prevented further clotting in Nixon for twenty years, and this demonstrates the competence and prudence of my judgment.

The long-distance diagnoses from the east and from university hospitals reached such a crescendo that Larry Altman in the *New York Times* wrote an extended essay entitled "Conflict on Care of Nixon: Town vs. Gown."[2] Altman described the resentment of the eastern medical establishment to Nixon's selection of a western community hospital in California, writing, "Conflicts between doctors practicing on a fee-for-service basis privately and those salaried by medical schools probably began when teaching institutions were first built. And regional differences undoubtedly have existed since the University of California, Stanford and other universities created medical schools in the West."[3] Altman continued: "When Mr. Nixon needed hospitalization for his phlebitis condition, he chose to go to a private community hospital—Memorial Hospital Medical Center—where his physician of long-standing, Dr. John C. Lungren, practiced. Mr. Nixon did not choose a university teaching hospital."[4]

I had been long associated with Memorial, formerly known as Seaside Hospital, first as a young physician returning from World War II to practice medicine in Long Beach: it was then located on Fourteen Street and Chestnut. In April 1959, Seaside Hospital became Memorial Hospital Medical Center and was relocated to a more central site on Atlantic Boulevard. Memorial grew rapidly to become a major regional medical center and the largest private hospital in the western United States. By 1974, it had 820 beds, 1,900 employees, and 600 staff physicians. Memorial's success reflects the great migration of young medical doctors and other health-care professionals to California after World War II.

Young physicians who had served in the war found the midwestern and eastern medical establishments closed for new entrants to private practice. Hence, many came west and many settled in southern California, including Long Beach, to begin private practice and raise families. By 1963, Memorial had reached a level of such stature in western medicine that an affiliation agreement with the University of California Irvine was reached whereby Irvine's medical students would examine Memorial patients in a clinical phase of the university medical school's curriculum.

Furthermore, professional jealousies and resentments also reigned within regions and faculties in western medicine itself. Altman explained: "Indeed, faculty members often speak of their institutions as the Harvard of the West. Yet the same academic rivalries exist within regions and even within the same localities elsewhere." This fact became apparent to me because, as Altman noted in his article, I had been privately criticized by UCLA physicians who "expressed resentment over how members of Mr. Nixon's medical team had cited their UCLA faculty titles." Altman wrote that the doctors were "embarrassed that the university had been tied to what they considered questionable medical decisions made in Mr. Nixon's case."

While I was indeed an associate clinical professor of medicine at UCLA, my primary commitment was to my private practice and my affiliation with Memorial Hospital Medical Center. If these doctors were criticizing anyone, it was their own university faculty since I was consulting with three of UCLA's most prominent professors of surgery: Dr. Wiley Barker, a nationally known vascular surgeon; Dr. William Longmeyer, the university's chief surgeon; and Dr. Donald Mulder, another prominent UCLA vascular surgeon.

In fact, it was Dr. Mulder who confirmed and supported our conservative approach to the problem of internal bleeding, which had caused Nixon's near-fatal shock after the operation. Rather than operate a second time to verify that the hemorrhaging had stopped, I ordered that Nixon receive whole-blood transfusions and platelet concentrates as necessary.

Altman also noted that I had been "criticized privately in medical circles" because I had not called on "experts in bleeding and clotting problems of the type that affected Mr. Nixon." Again, such criticism was unfounded. I had consulted with several experts, including Dr. William Smith, director of pharmacy at Memorial; Dr. Dennis Mackewicz, associate director of pharmacy at Memorial and assistant clinical professor of pharmacy at UCLA; Dr. James Baker, associate pathologist at Memorial (hematology section), and associate clinical professor of pathology at University of California Irvine; and Dr. Elmer Jennings, director of pathology at Memorial, associate clinical professor of pathology, University of California Irvine, and past president of the American Society of Clinical Pathologists.

I discharged Nixon from the hospital on November 14. Richard West and Kathy Burke of the *Los Angeles Times* described his departure: "Former president Richard M. Nixon, looking thin, pale and weak, left Long Beach Memorial Hospital after 23 days of treatment for phlebitis during which he nearly died from the effects of an operation."[5] Nixon, wearing pajamas and a bathrobe, had exited through a back service entrance, where a limousine transported him to his home in San Clemente.

When Nixon returned to La Casa Pacifica, his blood

pressure was erratic with random, abrupt, and rapid rises. This, in conjunction with the anticoagulants, compounded the danger of releasing a blood clot in his swollen left leg. Nixon's right lung was distorted by an accumulation of fluid, and a section of it held no air; his left leg required continual elevation.

Nixon was confronting death and life in *extremitas*, in fearsome despair and dread. Whether he would overcome such an overwhelming anguish of body and spirit was not assured and whether he would ever redeem his name and restore the honor lost by his complicity in Watergate seemed even less likely.

I gave my last news conference at Memorial shortly after bidding Nixon farewell as he departed with his Secret Service escort from the hospital's rear entrance. I felt that this conference should be more than a summary update on Nixon's current condition and the prognosis for his recovery. My experiences during the preceding two months had given me great concern about the responsibility of the media for fair reporting in a free society. I had seen my professional judgment called into question by the media. I was accused of perpetrating a "hoax" and building a "stonewall of silence" around Nixon to prevent him from testifying before Judge Sirica in the Watergate criminal trials. Federal prosecutors in Washington had challenged my credibility in open court. One reporter even feigned illness to see me and then asked audaciously what drugs Nixon was taking. Hate mail arrived every day from all parts of the world—some from physicians. My family had received obscene phone calls.

The period following Nixon's resignation was the darkest in his entire life. It was a time when every detail of his physical and mental condition was scrutinized by the media. The press, for the most part, was not interested in his

Nixon on State Street in Chicago—a classic campaign photo from the 1956 presidential election. Dr. Lungren stands in the Secret Service car behind Nixon's, taking a photograph of him. (Author's collection.)

(Above) Vice President Nixon and his senior campaign staff, 1956. Left to right in the front row: Herbert Klein, Pat Nixon, Richard Nixon, Raymond Arbuthnot, Edward Terrar. Back row: Warren Brock, Marjorie Peterson, James Bassett, Dr. John Lungren, H.R. (Bob) Haldeman, Jack Drown. (Associated Press.) *(Below)* Lungren family greets Vice President and Mrs. Nixon at Long Beach Airport during the fall 1956 election campaign. John Lungren Jr. is on the far left; Dan Lungren, future attorney general of California and U.S. representative, is standing beside him. (Author's collection.)

(Above) Dr. Lungren with Nixon on the 1968 campaign airplane. (Associated Press.) *(Below)* President-elect Nixon and Dr. Lungren answer reporters' questions on January 2, 1969, outside Long Beach Memorial Hospital Medical Center, where Nixon received his complete physical examination before the inauguration. (Philomene Royal, Memorial Hospital of Long Beach.)

(Above) August 13, 1969, photograph at a Los Angeles dinner honoring the Apollo 11 astronauts. From the left: Lorain Lungren, unidentified (holding glass), Rose Mary Woods, Paul Keyes with his wife. (Author's collection.) *(Below)* Nixon receives the American College of Cardiology's 1971 Humanitarian Award. Dr. Lungren is third from the left in the front row. (American College of Cardiology.)

(Above) Surrounded by police and Secret Service, Dr. Lungren escorts President Gerald Ford to visit Nixon at Long Beach Memorial Hospital. Nixon had almost died after surgery for phlebitic embolus. (Memorial Hospital of Long Beach.) *(Below)* The team of physicians who treated Nixon for phlebitis in October 1974. From the left: Dr. Lungren, former president Nixon, surgeon Eldon Hickman, M.D., and surgeon James Harper, M.D. (Memorial Hospital of Long Beach.)

(Above) Nixon shakes hands with Dr. Lungren after his twelve-day hospital stay in 1974. (Associated Press.) *(Below)* Photo of Nixon shaking hands with Dr. Lungren in San Clemente on December 1, 1976. Inscription: "To Dr. Jack Lungren, with deep appreciation for his superb medical attention and for his loyal friendship over the years—from Dick Nixon." (Colonel Jack Brennan.)

LA CASA PACIFICA
SAN CLEMENTE, CALIFORNIA

7-7-7 77

Dear Jack —

The unique combination of lucky 7's on this letterhead appropriately marks the day I received your announcement of your return to active practice.

I knew that your real heart would see you through the temporary damage to your physical heart.

Take good care of yourself so that you can continue to take good care of your patients.

Pat joins me in sending our congratulations & best wishes

Sincerely

Dick

Nixon's handwritten letter to Dr. Lungren, sent July 7, 1977, welcoming him back to medical practice after his recovery from a heart attack. (Author's collection.)

Dinner for the Nixon Library Fund in December 1988. From the left: Lorain Lungren, Dr. Lungren, Julie Nixon Eisenhower, Henry Kissinger. (Richard Nixon Library & Birthplace.)

physical problems but wanted to know only when he would be able to return to Washington to testify.

On the positive side, however, there were reporters who were more objective, and their inquiries were more relevant. There were two journalists in particular for whom I had immense respect because of their thorough professionalism, integrity, and accuracy. Lawrence Altman, M.D., medical correspondent for the *New York Times,* was helpful and decisive in his questions and reporting. Undoubtedly, his medical expertise contributed to his superior coverage of Nixon's medical condition. The second journalist whose judgment I enjoyed and respected was Roy Neal, the correspondent for NBC News. Neal was always objective in his reporting of my press conferences. In a letter to me dated September 25, 1974, Neal wrote, "In retrospect, I feel that we were able to describe Mr. Nixon's condition accurately and it was due to your efforts. If we didn't, it certainly was not your fault!" He also told me that NBC News anchor John Chancellor misquoted him by saying that Nixon was "in heavy pain," the "direct opposite" of what Neal told NBC editors in New York. Neal asked for an immediate retraction from his editors. Dr. Altman requested that a similar misquotation of one of my statements in the *News York Times* be retracted.

Both Altman and Neal were sensitive to the inviolable privilege of privacy between physician and patient. On September 18, 1974, Altman wrote me, "I fully appreciate the delicate balance between the confidentiality of the patient-doctor relationship and the public's right to know." Neal was instrumental in drafting a letter from the press corps, sent October 24, requesting me to hold an additional news conference with a pooled panel of reporters to clarify the possibility of surgery for Nixon. In the letter the reporters stated that Nixon's condition was too much a matter of genuine public concern to be totally sheltered under the normal doctor-patient relationship, and they urged me to make myself available as "the best way to head off future speculative reporting."

In response to the reporters' request, I gave a news conference on October 27, beginning with a brief summary of Nixon's current condition. Then I addressed the assembled media, which numbered over two hundred reporters from all over the world.

> Ladies and gentleman: Before we open the discussion to questions, I have a few off-the-record personal remarks that I would like to make. While I am hopeful that this will be my last news conference with you, I want to say that I have enjoyed meeting with you during the last two months. I have developed a great amount of respect for many members of your profession.
>
> However, there are some newsmen and their editors who have wanted to turn the illness of the former president of the United States into a political football. I consider this to be a lamentable action, unworthy of a profession that claims to possess objectivity.
>
> I would like to review briefly with you two important aspects of this prolonged illness: one, the certified and well-trained team of physicians, nurses, and health professionals who played a vital role in the care of the patient; and two, the numerous factors of the illness itself. I feel very strongly that former President Nixon has been treated by the highest caliber of western medicine. Both Dr. Hickman and I would at this time like to express publicly our deep appreciation to all of the individuals who offered their expertise and dedication.

For a moment, let us just review the so-called "hoax" or—as some individuals would like to characterize it—"put on" illness of the former president of the United States. Let us review his illness from the beginning, including all the complications he possibly has undergone: four or perhaps five bouts of active phlebitis with or without embolism in the left leg and left pelvis; one instance of pulmonary embolus; surgery performed in an effort to prevent a fresh clot formation from moving to the lung; postoperative retroperitoneal hemorrhage with vascular shock necessitating counter-shock measures, including blood and platelet transfusions; development of postoperative adelctisis and pneumanitis; development of postoperative pleural effusion; potential of hepatitis; and potential of possible postphlebitic syndrome. This, gentlemen and ladies, is the saga of the "hoax" of the former president's illness.

I knew that allegations of a hoax would not subside unless the Sirica panel vindicated my medical judgment. Dr. Hufnagel called me on Monday, November 18. "John," he said, "I know you are wondering why I accepted this appointment, especially as chairman of the panel. I felt your medical judgment deserved fair and objective evaluation in light of the unfair criticism you have received from the press and our own profession." He continued, "You and I have known each other a long time since we were students at Notre Dame. I know your integrity and know your judgment has been accurate and unbiased."

"I am grateful, Charlie," I replied. "Your concern reflects the sense of justice and true community Notre Dame gave us." In this context, I was referring not merely to a sense of fraternity and fair play, so well known in American universities, but to a deeper sense of community and shared spiritual values.

Hufnagel then told me that panel member Dr. Richard Starr Ross was being inducted as president of the American Heart Association in Dallas that week, making it impossible for the panel to examine Nixon before the following Monday. Hufnagel also said that he knew that I had planned a vacation with my wife during this period. I explained that everything was arranged for the panel's visit and that Dr. Eldon Hickman, who performed Nixon's surgery, would represent me during the consultation and examination.

I outlined the ground rules for the examination, including the stipulation that Nixon's medical records could be examined only in the presence of Nixon's physician (in this case Dr. Hickman) and the Secret Service. I told him that this precaution was necessary not only from a standpoint of medical privacy but also because of the break-in at my office in Long Beach (see appendix, p. 186).

"John, I just can't believe that this could happen," Hufnagel said incredulously.

"Charlie," I responded, "don't be so naïve. In fact, it didn't stop there. My own family has been harassed, including my daughter Loretta studying at St. Mary's College, who received an obscene phone call."

I cautioned Hufnagel that both Nixon and his wife were opposed to the intrusion into their privacy caused by Sirica's order. Furthermore, the Nixons viewed the Sirica panel as an insult to me and my colleagues, who had saved Nixon's life and were restoring his health. Hufnagel replied that the panel was composed of honorable, ethical physicians who would conduct the examination in a dignified, nonintrusive manner. He said that the examination would be brief, no longer than ten minutes, giving the panel ample time to assess Nixon's condition. I then gave Hufnagel Dr. Hickman's phone number to coordinate the examination. On the morning of November 25, 1975, the panel of physicians appointed by Judge Sirica arrived at Long Beach Memorial Hospital Medical Center to meet with Dr. Eldon Hickman, Nixon's surgeon, whom I had directed to accompany the panel to San Clemente in my absence. An awkward incident occurred immediately upon their arrival. The panel members had forgotten to bring the legal documents signed by Judge Sirica authorizing their examination. After a series of phone calls, including one to San Clemente, some consideration was given to postponing the examination, but then Dr. Hickman took charge of the situation. He suggested that the panel proceed to San Clemente as planned, since it would make for a cooperative, good-faith relationship. He reasoned that the examination would eventually take place in any case.

Aware of the panel's impending visit, the media requested a press conference with the panel at Memorial before it left for San Clemente. The three physicians all agreed that such a conference was premature and inappropriate. Memorial's public-relations staff handled the situation well, and a press conference was avoided. Before leaving, the panel reviewed all of Nixon's medical records, including the venogram of Nixon's phlebitic leg, and asked Dr. Hickman basic questions about Nixon's progress and condition. Satisfied with this phase of the medical evaluation, the three physicians and Dr. Hickman left the hospital for San Clemente in several cars, escorted by Secret Service agents. As they traveled south on the San Diego Freeway, their convoy was trailed by press cars, windows down and cameras rolling.

The convoy entered La Casa Pacifica's gate uneventfully, and Dr. Hickman introduced the physicians to the Secret Service agents, who escorted them and Dr. Hickman to Nixon's residence. Dr. Hickman was met at the door by a Nixon aide; initial introductions were made, and then all entered the bedroom. Nixon was in bed wearing pajamas and a robe. Dr. Hickman introduced the panel to Nixon and reviewed the evaluation procedures, which consisted of direct questions and a physical examination.

Prior to the formal examination, casual conversation between Nixon and the physicians helped to diminish the awkward, tense nature of the court-ordered inquiry. Dr. Richard Ross noted an engraved jewelry box on Nixon's bedside table and said he had been presented a similar box while he was a visiting cardiologist in Russia two years earlier. This led to additional conversation regarding Russia, problems of travel, and related matters. While the conversation was generally nonpolitical, there was also discussion of President Ford's arms-limitation initiatives with the Soviet Union. Since one of the physicians was a Quaker, there was further conversation regarding Nixon's Quaker background. Dr. Hickman recalls, "All in all, it was a friendly, relaxed introduction."

The physicians in turn questioned Nixon, who described his previous history of phlebitis, describing how painfully swollen his left leg had been during his visit to Egypt in June 1974. Nixon explained that after the resignation in September he began noticing thigh pain as well as additional pain in his lower left leg. Nixon recounted the events leading to his phone call in September to request that I take care of him and his subsequent admission to the hospital. He told the panel that it was painful to have a venogram and that the anticoagulant Heparin drip he was receiving made it difficult to sleep. The physicians asked additional questions about the two hospitalizations. Nixon replied that he did not remember many details about the second hospitalization in October after losing consciousness in the postoperative recovery room. Nixon said that he was happy to be home and that he had very little pain in his leg but that it was still swollen. He wore an elastic support-stocking at all times except when in bed. Nixon complained of a poor appetite and some weight loss. He made a habit of attempting to walk once or twice a day—between one hundred and two hundred yards at a time—but did so with difficulty because he tired very easily. He told the panel that he slept eight to twelve hours a night and that his medication included a blood-pressure pill, Valium, Dalmain, and Coumadin. Additional questions were asked about the mild hypertension that I had noted during his hospitalization. Nixon did not remember being diagnosed for hypertension prior to this illness but did recall being told that he had a slightly elevated cholesterol level.

Each physician in turn examined Nixon, who was cooperative although he appeared to be slightly annoyed by the procedure. Dr. Ross, a cardiologist, examined Nixon's heart, lungs, and neck, and he took his blood pressure five or six times standing, sitting, and lying down. Dr. Spitell examined Nixon's abdomen and lower extremities, measuring his left calf as being one and a half inches larger than the right. Dr. Hufnagel, a cardiovascular surgeon, examined Nixon's left lower leg with a Doppler machine to evaluate his arterial and venous circulation.

Satisfied that their examination was complete, the physicians took leave of Nixon with friendly farewells. The panel's examination had taken an hour. The Secret Service escorted the panel and Dr. Hickman back to Long Beach Memorial Hospital, where the three physicians went their separate ways to prepare medical evaluations and recommendations for Judge Sirica.

On November 30, on board a cruise ship in the Mediterranean, I heard a UPI dispatch on the ship's radio report that the Sirica panel had unequivocally affirmed my medical judgment. Without reservation, the panel concluded that Nixon was not physically capable of giving testimony at the Watergate trial either in person in Washington, D.C., or by videotape in San Clemente before February 1975. The panel also concluded that Nixon was physically incapable of giving a written deposition until January.

Robert L. Jackson noted in the *Los Angeles Times* that the report included the panel's conclusions but no supporting medical data. As panel chairman, Dr. Hufnagel explained the situation in a transmittal letter to Judge Sirica: "If required by the court, the panel can submit the medical reasons and data upon which it based its report. This would involve specific information, regarding his condition, which we have been instructed is confidential." Hufnagel stated that he and his two colleagues firmly believed in the ethics of medical privacy. Even the resigned former president, while still a public figure, was entitled to a threshold of privacy that should not be crossed. The panel report stated that Nixon was "not presently able" to travel to Washington, D.C., to testify, noting, "If recovery proceeds at the anticipated rate, and there are no further complications, we would estimate that such a trip should be possible by February 16, 1975."[6]

The panel gave February 2 as the date for Nixon's earliest possible testimony in a California courtroom and January 6 as the date for videotape testimony from La Casa Pacifica. The panel declared that Nixon should be given the opportunity for rest between sessions of testimony and that a physician should be in attendance during the taking of a deposition.

Jackson also reported that Judge Sirica had contemplated moving the trial temporarily to California to obtain Nixon's testimony. In the end, however, Sirica took no action, for the panel's report was conclusive in its assessment of the serious threat to Nixon's health were he to be compelled to testify before he had recovered.

In the *New York Times,* Lawrence K. Altman questioned Hufnagel's reference to confidentiality, writing that there was irony in protecting Nixon's privacy in light of the conduct of the Nixon White House during Watergate. Altman referred to the so-called special unit known as the "plumbers" which broke into the office of the former psychiatrist of Daniel Ellsberg, who himself had violated national security in publishing the classified Pentagon Papers. Altman then proceeded to cast doubt on the panel's integrity:[7]

> Many people, doctors included, have expressed amazement at how the health of a man could deteriorate so rapidly. While President, Mr. Nixon prided himself on his vigor and stamina. But Dr. Hufnagel has declined to answer the basic question of how the panel went about its business. He declined on the ground that by providing such information he would be violating the confidential nature of the doctor-patient relationship.
>
> Dr. Hufnagel has said that the panel approached the problem as if it were a case of disability. In other words, he indicated that the panel had tried to determine when Mr. Nixon would be fit to return to work.
>
> What job? What criteria do doctors have for determining the workloads of former Presidents or the average person who faces legal problems?
>
> Did the doctors ask Mr. Nixon to walk across his bedroom at his San Clemente, Calif. estate to

determine how fatigued such physical exercise would make him? Did they measure his blood pressure when they arrived and then repeat the test just before they left to determine the degree of stress their short visit caused the former President? Did the panel call a psychiatrist?[8]

Altman knew these were rhetorical questions. Earlier in his article, he had stated the reason why Hufnagel had invoked the ethic of confidentiality in the first place—"the sanctity of the patient doctor relationship, a fundamental principle upon which medicine is practiced."

Ray Price, Nixon's chief speechwriter in the White House, described Nixon's appearance more than a month after Hufnagel's statement. It was a Sunday, and Nixon had invited Price to have dinner with Pat and himself. "When I arrived for dinner, it was the first time I had seen him since before that brush with death three months earlier," Price wrote. "He was still thin, gaunt, haggard and moving with evident difficulty. Mrs. Nixon took me aside, and told me enthusiastically that he had improved 'a hundred percent' in just the past week. He himself was proud to be getting his weight back at last. I wondered at what sort of ghost he must have been the week before, and the week before that."[9]

Dr. Hickman made two or three more visits to San Clemente to monitor Nixon's recovery while I was on vacation. On one occasion, after receiving permission from Nixon's staff, Dr. Hickman brought his wife, Jerry. Nixon greeted Dr. Hickman and his wife in his living room, and they had a friendly conversation about their children. Nixon learned that Jerry Hickman had developed severe hypertension and vascular disease at a young age. Nixon was quite interested in discussing medical issues, including hypertension. After the conversation ended, Dr. Hickman examined Nixon and found his progress to be satisfactory.

Dr. Hickman never saw Nixon again after I resumed my visits to San Clemente and there was no further need of surgical consultation. Yet when Jerry Hickman died due to complications from her premature cardiovascular hypertensive disease in January 1976, Nixon called Dr. Hickman to offer his condolences and reiterate his appreciation for his surgical care. Dr. Hickman recalled that he was "quite honored and gratified to hear directly from the former president."

After returning from my three-week vacation on Friday, December 13, I called Nixon on the following Sunday to review his progress. Nixon told me that he had gained some weight and felt somewhat stronger. We discussed the Sirica panel's examination and its report affirming my medical judgment. Nixon said that the three physicians had acted in a very professional manner. However, he believed that they had bent over backwards to stay nonpolitical so that they would not be perceived as having a political bias as was being alleged in some quarters. I had received a number of letters and telegrams from physicians and citizens across the country stating that Sirica had politicized a medical issue. These letters of support only added to the vindication I felt at receiving the panel's approval.

10

Nixon, Sinatra, Dreyfus

THE FOLLOWING FRIDAY I was to return to La Casa Pacifica at 3:00 P.M. I received a call from Colonel Brennan asking if I could come a half-hour later since Nixon had scheduled a lunch with Frank Sinatra. Arriving at 3:30 P.M., I immediately noticed Sinatra's private helicopter on the pad where *Marine One* had landed so many times. In the parking area, I saw a blue Cadillac with the initials PWK. The initials belonged to Paul Keyes, an aggressive and likable Hollywood television producer with whom I was acquainted through mutual friends. Manola Sanchez, after greeting me, told me that while he believed Nixon was improved, he seemed rather depressed at times. He had noticed this particularly after Nixon had received a recent phone call from Julie. Manola hinted at a minor domestic dispute. I knew of Nixon's passion, intense affection, and deep love for his family, so I was not surprised at Manola's observation. Manola also related that Nixon's appetite had improved and that Mrs. Nixon was actively involved in gardening and managing various household activities on the estate. Manola escorted me into the living room, where Nixon, Sinatra, and Keyes were seated and engaged in conversation.

I greeted Nixon and Keyes, and the former president immediately introduced me to Sinatra. We shook hands, and Sinatra congratulated me on my care of Nixon. Sinatra was most pleasant, exuding tremendous self-confidence. It was interesting and exciting to meet Sinatra, the legendary singer who was the definitive interpreter of American popular song in the twentieth century. Yet I wondered why Nixon, who preferred intellectual discussion of such topics as the views of Aquinas and Augustine on the "just war," enjoyed chatting with Hollywood celebrities. Nixon and Sinatra probably had less in common than the two protagonists in the Sinatra song "Strangers in the Night." In addition, Sinatra had supported John F. Kennedy against Nixon in 1960.

After Sinatra and Keyes left, Nixon and I went into his bedroom for an examination. I found his blood pressure to be normal, although medical corpsman Dunn told me that Nixon's diastolic pressure had been elevated during the last few weeks. Nixon and I spoke about the Watergate trial, of his willingness to testify once he felt physically up to it, and the possibility of a mistrial; we wished each other's families a happy holiday season.

I told Nixon that Colonel Brennan wanted to see me, so we drove over to the old Western White House compound. We went to Brennan's office and immediately began a discussion of Nixon's medical and hospitalization expenses. Brennan said that Nixon wanted to know the total cost since he had signed a contract for his book and had received an advance payment. Brennan explained that Nixon was anxious to know the total amount before the first of the year since, if it were feasible, he wanted to make a sizable contribution to Long Beach Memorial Hospital Medical Center. Colonel Brennan said the bill for the first hospitalization was $4,800, which had been paid; they had just received the second bill for $7,800, which Nixon thought was reasonable. I informed him that I had checked with the hospital business manager and confirmed that that was the total bill. As for the doctors, I reported that all had submitted their bills except me and that mine would be submitted early the following week.

Another matter discussed was the decision by the General Services Administration, under pressure by vindictive congressmen, to reassign Chief Dunn to Camp Pendleton as his primary duty and reduce his care of Nixon to a secondary responsibility. As a medical doctor, I viewed Chief Dunn as indispensable to the monitoring of Nixon's health and believed that reassigning him to Camp Pendleton was irresponsible and potentially prejudicial to Nixon's health. Nixon noted with evident irritation to Brennan and me that Harry Truman had two medical corpsmen assigned to him for life and that Lyndon Johnson had four corpsmen for life, three for himself and one for his wife. "The powers that be in Washington will pick my bones a little more," Nixon said sardonically, "unless you feel for health reasons the Chief should stay on and which would require an affidavit to that effect." Nixon then expressed his frustration with the restricted regimen of recovery: "I am used to working at 150 percent, and I need to get to work on the book."

On January 5, 1975, I submitted to the Congress and the General Services Administration the following affidavit: "The former President of the United States has been and still is a patient under my care. At the present time and for an undetermined period in the future it is my professional judgment that the attendance of a knowledgeable paramedic should be available to the patient on a 24-hour basis. His duties, in addition to rendering possible emergency care, include the drawing of blood, recording of vital signs and the delivery of periodic medical reports to me, the attending physician. The presence of this individual is particularly important during the present period of recovery while the former President is being administered anticoagulation therapy." The Congress and GSA ignored my affidavit and professional judgment. Chief Dunn was reassigned to Camp Pendleton and was able to monitor Nixon on only a limited basis. Had Nixon developed further complications in his anticoagulation therapy, such as internal bleeding or another blood clot, he could very well have died. It is a serious matter to engage in political recriminations and vindictive reprisals when a human life is at stake.

During one of our conversations, Nixon told me of a phone call he had received from Jack Dreyfus, the founder of the multibillion-dollar Dreyfus investment fund and one of America's wealthiest persons. Dreyfus had taken an almost messianic interest in Dilantin, a drug which purportedly could aid depression and enhance physical and mental well-being. Dreyfus was attempting to persuade Nixon to use the drug.

Dilantin, dyphenylhydantoin or DPH, is a drug that has proved successful in treating epilepsy and heart arrhythmias but also has been found beneficial in addressing clinical depression. I considered using Dilantin for Nixon's depression during his recovery but decided against it because I had my own rigorous and structured rehabilitation regimen planned. The regimen emphasized therapeutic thresholds that were intellectual, physical, and social in nature, such as writing books, exercise (golf and swimming), and social involvement.

Nixon had to address these thresholds actively rather than depending on a passive drug therapy, which would tend to dominate the process of recovery. As an internist, I understood very well that pharmacological therapy for depression is often the only way to extricate a patient from the dangerous courses the mind may take. However, in Nixon's case, I knew that restoration of his well-being required the total reengagement of his mental and physical faculties.

Dreyfus wrote me on January 6, 1975, outlining the pharmacological benefits of the drug in an attempt to persuade me to give it to Nixon:[1]

> Dear Dr. Lungren:
>
> President Nixon asked me to send you the enclosed material. We are completing another bibliography and review of diphenylhydantoin to be called "DPH, 1975" which will be a supplement to the enclosed book. It will contain a great amount of additional clinical and basic mechanisms evidence of the benefits and safety of DPH.
>
> . . . We have already studied the literature with encouraging results, but as a further precaution we are checking with physicians at leading hospitals who have had wide experience with DPH.
>
> Because of the fact that the drug money which had the early patents on diphenylhydantoin has chronic pernicious apatheticus, and the Food and Drug Administration is empowered only to act in the negative, the remarkable benefits of this substance have been hidden from the general public. Fortunately, this is rapidly changing, as the enclosed Lee survey of the current uses to which physicians are putting DPH will show.

I would like to take this chance, as a friend
of the President, to tell you how deeply I
appreciate your fine work in bringing him
through a most serious time.

With best regards,

Jack Dreyfus

Dilantin was manufactured in the laboratories of Warner-Lambert, a company whose president, Elmer Bobst, was one of Nixon's closest friends. Nixon enjoyed the friendship of powerful men of accomplishment in the business world, including Dreyfus and Bobst. I believe he admired their practical and tenacious attitude in achieving success, a down-to-earth pragmatism in day-to-day affairs that brought them the financial security that Nixon had never known.

11

Habeas Corpus: Nixon on Watergate and Vietnam

WATERGATE AND VIETNAM—these cardinal events ultimately destroyed Richard Nixon's presidency. I discussed Watergate and Vietnam innumerable times with Nixon for several months of grave illness beginning in September 1974 and through the years of rehabilitation and recovery at La Casa Pacifica (1974–1980). On occasion, Pat Nixon would join in the discussions.

In early January of 1975, I drove to San Clemente to give Nixon a physical examination and visit with him. I found him adhering to my prescribed regimen of a few hours of concentration followed by a rest period. Nixon told that me he tired easily. Nevertheless, we engaged in an uninhibited conversation over a wide range of subjects, including the Watergate break-in, the Pentagon Papers, Daniel Ellsberg, the Kennedys, the Supreme Court, and the aberrant conduct of Nixon's two immediate predecessors. We also discussed football—the elegant offenses of Notre Dame coach Ara Paraseghian, the Pittsburgh Steelers' chances in the Super Bowl, the prowess of Rocky Bleier, the Steeler running-back from Notre Dame, and the tenacity of Steeler owner Art Rooney.

Our conversation then turned to more serious matters. I asked Nixon about the Watergate trial verdicts delivered on New Year's Day. "Jack," he promptly answered, "I felt very sorry about the guilty verdicts. You know the appeals will last at least a year or more. I am still worried about other potential investigations by the special prosecutor. However, I feel it will be a minor issue—now that the 'big fish' have been caught in the net." The "big fish" Nixon referred to were H.R. Haldeman, chief of staff; John Ehrlichman, domestic policy adviser; John Dean, White House counsel; and John Mitchell, attorney general. Nixon continued:

> Jack, I am alarmed about the double standard that has been applied to all the hearings and the political motivation behind the Watergate affair. When you know the severe excesses carried out by my predecessors—and the tapes, my constitutional rights were violated when the tapes were subpoenaed—they were in effect my private papers.
>
> We must remember that "executive privileges" were supported and lauded by the liberal press in the Truman, JFK, LBJ, and Eisenhower administrations. The Democrat majority in Congress during those years felt that "executive privileges" by the President of the United States should be honored and respected.
>
> A Democrat majority in Congress and the judicial system reversed the sanctity of executive privilege, a privilege first advanced by Thomas Jefferson in 1806. Jefferson refused to comply with subpoena, saying that the leading principle

of our Constitution was the independence of the
legislative, judicial, and executive branches of
government. This is exactly my position too.

The Supreme Court has affirmed executive privilege as constitutional.[1] For the rest of his life Nixon believed that the
tapes were his own private conversations, that executive
privilege did apply, that the conversations on the tapes were
taken out of context and deliberately distorted by the media, the Democrats, and antiwar activists to force his impeachment.

"Jack, I never knew about the Watergate break-in incident until after it occurred," Nixon said emphatically. "I
did not order the break-in or even contemplate such in-
sanely stupid actions. And there's no viable evidence, after
millions spent by Watergate investigators, that I was involved." Nixon continued: "The Watergate break-in was fool-
ish, unnecessary and stupid. This is why I say that my actions
regarding the attempted cover-up were politically legal but
perhaps morally wrong. However, the political acts of my
predecessors, JFK and LBJ, established a pattern of behavior that was 'apresidential' and often worse than any act in
my entire administration. I am referring to events like the
Bay of Pigs disaster for Kennedy and the Bobby Baker affair for Johnson."

On one occasion, after Nixon's memoirs were published, Nixon and I discussed Daniel Ellsberg and the Pentagon Papers. Daniel Ellsberg, a policy analyst at the Rand
Corporation, became an antiwar activist and secretly pho-
tocopied a classified political and historical study about U.S.
involvement in Vietnam. Ellsberg gave the photocopies to
the *New York Times,* which published them as the Pentagon
Papers. A 6-3 Supreme Court decision permitted the release of the papers.[2]

"Dick, you know that the media has made the general public believe that you ordered a break-in at the Brookings Institution?" I asked. "Jack, this allegation is a total lie! I have explained this in detail in my memoirs. Let me summarize for you: I knew that in various interviews Ellsberg had said that he was convinced that I intended to escalate the war rather than pull troops out of Vietnam," Nixon began. "Well, Ellsberg didn't know what the hell he was talking about. I had to end this war if only because it was so tragically, wastefully, and ineptly conducted by Johnson and the Democrats," Nixon said. "I couldn't expect young men to fight and die due to the fruitless prosecution of a war without any discernible objectives. And with no goddamn plan to end it! Jack, when I walked into the Oval Office on January 20th I found nothing from my predecessor—no plans, no contingencies, no options, no scenarios—regarding what to do in Vietnam," Nixon told me. He continued:

> I also knew that during his years at the Defense Department, Ellsberg had access to some of the most sensitive information in the entire government. Imagine my reaction when I was told that the highly classified bombing halt material and other top secret documents had been taken to Brookings.
>
> The aftershock of publishing the Pentagon Papers, all of the uncertainty following, the renewed criticism of the war—this produced my interest in President Johnson's bombing halt file. When I was told it was still at Brookings, I was furious and frustrated. It seemed absurd!—I could not accept that we had lost so much control over the workings of government we had been elected to run.

I saw absolutely no reason for that report to be at Brookings and said I wanted it back right away—even if it meant having to get it surreptitiously. The fact is there was no break-in at the Brookings Institution.

Nixon's anger was also compounded by the Supreme Court's decision to allow the publisher and editors of the *New York Times* to print the Pentagon Papers. What really disturbed Nixon about the *New York Times* publishing the Pentagon Papers was its effect on the peace Nixon was trying to negotiate to end the war. "The release of the Pentagon Papers to the public at this time probably hampered the peace offer being made to North Vietnam," Nixon said.

Nixon reminded me of what faced him following his inauguration in January 1969: "I had to work with both Houses of Congress in the hands of hostile Democrats. Add to that I was in constant combat with the Supreme Court, led by Chief Justice Earl Warren, who really should have been a Democrat with his liberal stripes. I also had to battle three more justices, liberal Democratic members of the Supreme Court, Brennan, Marshall, and Douglas, all of whose favorite judicial pastime was to rewrite the Constitution. And, Jack, don't forget I always had the Kennedy machine nipping at my heels. They were a gang of formidable foes, ever opposed to me, who had never fully recovered from the shock that I had become the thirty-seventh president of the United States."

Then Nixon spoke of the heavy burden of a war he believed he carried as president: "People forget I was a war president! I was engaged with dedicated enemy forces whose successful propaganda had split the nation in two as much as Lincoln prosecuted the Civil War to preserve a divided nation. Remember, Jack, Lincoln suspended habeas corpus, one of the chief constitutional guarantees of our civil liberties," Nixon declared.

Nixon stressed that his own motivation derived from Lincoln's pragmatic reasoning for suspension of habeas corpus and his famous rhetorical question: "Are all the laws but one to go unexecuted, and the Government go to pieces lest one be violated?" According to Nixon, he had faced the same intractable issues as Lincoln: rebellious dissidents within the government and radical protestors in the streets. On April 19, 1861, a mob of twenty thousand confederate sympathizers cheering for Jefferson Davis attacked Union troops at two Baltimore railroad stations by throwing paving stones. Soldiers shot into the crowd, killing four civilians; protestors shot back, killing two soldiers. Further encounters ensued, and sixteen persons were killed, twelve civilians and four soldiers. This incident directly led to Lincoln's decision to suspend habeas corpus.[3] In a speech near the end of the war, Lincoln assessed the influence of "rebel sympathizers." "Under cover of 'Liberty of speech,' 'Liberty of the press,' and 'habeas corpus,' they hoped to keep on foot amongst us a most efficient corps of spies, informers, suppliers and aiders and abettors of their cause in a thousand ways."[4]

Nine months into Nixon's presidency, antiwar protests were approaching proportions similar to those which had bedeviled President Johnson and eventually forced him from office. Nixon believed the antiwar movement remained unscrutinized by an American media that, in fact, was sympathetic to the protester's ultimate aim of discrediting his administration. He believed that these forces aligned with a Democratic Congress to disable and eventually destroy his presidency.

Tragically, in retaliation Nixon decided to scrutinize his own opponents without restraint. When the Pentagon Papers were published, Nixon ordered a "plumbers'" unit to be formed to prevent intelligence leaks from the White House. Of course, this was the group that made the infamous entry into Democratic National Headquarters at Watergate.

Washington Post columnist and political analyst David Broder believed there was a concerted effort to destroy the Nixon presidency by an alignment of protestors, liberals in Congress, and media. "The anti-war movement was trying to break the President," Broder wrote. He stated that the very politicians and liberal press who drove President Johnson out of office were actively attempting to do the same to President Nixon. "'Impeach him.' Is that not really the proper course, rather than destroying his capacity to lead, while leaving him in office . . . rather than leaving the nation with a broken President at its head for three years?" Broder asked.

It was here—at this catastrophic conjunction between the moral and political disasters of Vietnam and Watergate— that the Nixon presidency ended. The majesty of the nation's common purpose was left greatly diminished as the two catastrophes became one cataclysm.

12

Nixon and the Jews

NIXON HAD STRONG FEELINGS and often privately expressed them in profane ways; when these comments became public on the Watergate tapes, his reputation for tolerance and fairness was damaged. One area of sustained debate and controversy that pursued Nixon during his political life was his relationship with Jews and the Jewish community.

While Nixon never made any remarks that could be construed as anti-Semitic in my presence, I know that he believed that he had been treated unfairly by some members of the American Jewish community. Nixon also asked similar questions regarding the unfairness of other groups who opposed his policies and political strategies in ways that were never charming.

During the 1968 presidential campaign, I was aware that Nixon wondered why a large segment of the Jewish electorate failed to support his candidacy, particularly the many successful, brilliant Hollywood impresarios, film studio owners, producers, writers, and directors who had Jewish ancestry. Later, this subject was no longer an issue and was apparently forgotten for the remainder of the campaign.

When agitated about such issues, Nixon would use offensive language. Some of these regrettable remarks had been recorded on the tapes that were released in October 1999. For example, in a 1971 conversation, Nixon calls Max Frankel, then *New York Times* Washington bureau chief, "that damned Jew Frankel." As the *New York Times* former executive editor, Frankel played a pivotal role in angering Nixon by publishing the Pentagon Papers. In February 1972, Nixon expressed his anger by permitting only one *New York Times* reporter to cover his historic trip to China in February 1972; other newspapers had at least three reporters. Ironically, Frankel's superior reporting on the trip won a Pulitzer prize for the *New York Times*. Frankel simply outworked, outwalked, and outwrote the more than three thousand journalists covering the story, and he gave Nixon's diplomatic achievement a perspective worthy of its historic magnitude.[1]

My own view is that Nixon's taped comments about Jews are indefensible, even if done in private "to blow off steam." Paradoxically, Nixon's public conduct toward the Jewish community indicates that he held the Jewish faith, members of the Jewish community, and Israel in the highest regard. Four critical positions in the Nixon White House were held by Jews appointed by President Nixon: Henry Kissinger, national security adviser and secretary of state; William Safire, speechwriter; Leonard Garment, liaison to the arts community and to the Jewish community; and Alan Greenspan, chairman of the Council of Economic Advisers.

It was Nixon who saved Israel during the October 1973 Yom Kippur War when Egypt struck Israel with blinding surprise. Nixon once told me: "During my Presidential years, Jack, do not forget my order for an alert and total airlift to Israel during the Yom Kippur War. My actions were praised in Israel and should have been in most segments of the Jewish community in America." Nixon alone favored aiding Israel with full military assistance, and he overruled nearly all of his advisers, including Henry Kissinger, the Pentagon, and the State Department. On October 12 and 13, 1973, Nixon ordered air force cargo planes to transport tanks, Sidewinder missiles, and other military equipment directly to Israel: "Goddamn it . . . use every one we have!" Nixon declared. "Tell them to send everything that can fly!"[2]

Nixon's alleged anti-Semitism always perplexed me, since I had never heard Nixon speak in that manner in my presence. We had discussed the issue several times during the course of his rehabilitation, but only indirectly, treating it as merely another allegation. When I visited Nixon to check his progress on January 2, 1975, I felt it would be an opportune time to ask him about the allegations in the press, inasmuch as Henry Kissinger was coming to see Nixon for the first time since his resignation. During our conversation that day I asked, "Dick, what about the allegations of anti-Semitism that have persisted during your political career?" Wasting no words, Nixon answered: "Jack, you know that prejudice of any degree has never been permitted in the Quaker belief; and as I grow older, my Quaker background lights up—or maybe, like I once said to you, I think I could become a Catholic." I do not believe Nixon was being disingenuous with me. I knew Nixon well enough to know these words were genuine and unaffected. In his heart of hearts, Nixon was truly influenced by his mother's Quaker heritage of peace and tolerance; and Nixon's attraction to Catholicism was not casual but spiritually strong.

13

Nixon and Kissinger

MY NEXT VISIT TO LA CASA PACIFICA was on January 24, 1975. I was directed by Secret Service to the office compound of the former Western White House, where I found Nixon dressed in a sports outfit and looking better than he had in a long time. Nixon's color was returning; his physical stamina and mental attitude seemed much improved. However, I was very seriously concerned about the ultimate outcome of Nixon's turbulent inner struggle and shattering confrontation with the dark forces of despair.

For even after my vindication by the Sirica panel, which meant that Nixon did not have to go to Washington to testify at the Watergate trial, he was still close to giving up on himself, on life, on the future. Nixon had never before experienced this feeling, this emotional and psychic disintegration. Always before, he had come back from defeat and fought hard all the way. Now the resilience, the fight, the 150 percent were slipping away. Nixon was descending into dark despair, a dangerous slide that often proves irreversible.

As an internist and a cardiologist, I had witnessed the collapse of the will to live in many patients, and I knew that mental and physical disintegration would soon follow. An ever-enveloping and deepening ennui possesses the patient, which is the usual prelude to death. The more I practiced medicine, the more I marveled at the mysterious, symbiotic unity of the mind and body, so fatefully interwoven.

Nixon described what he felt upon hearing the news that the Sirica medical panel had affirmed my judgment that his condition precluded traveling to Washington and testifying at the Watergate trial. Instead of exhilaration at the decision, Nixon felt only wrenching enervation and ennui. Nixon described his depression as a disintegration of the will to live by which his purpose in life was lost and his enthusiasm for achievement exhausted: "I did not get the lift that I should have when I received the news that I would not have to go to Washington. For the first time in my life, I was a physical wreck; I was emotionally drained; I was mentally burned out. This time, as compared with other crises I had endured, I could see no reason to live, no cause to fight for. Unless a person has a reason to live for other than himself, he will die first mentally, then emotionally, then physically."[1]

As I began to examine Nixon's left leg, he noted that Kissinger would be arriving shortly. I decided that with Kissinger's impending visit it would be a good time to take Nixon's blood pressure for my overall assessment of his physical and mental progress. I knew that Nixon was looking forward to Kissinger's visit; Kissinger was one of the few confidantes who was an intellectual peer with whom he could discuss the course of historical development and its intersection with politics and diplomacy. Nixon saw in Kissinger an intellectual companion with whom he could engage in intellectual duals.

Nixon was familiar with Kissinger's doctoral dissertation, which was eventually published as *The World Restored: Metternich, Castlereagh, and the Problems of Peace, 1812–22*, a prescient and elegant study of the balance of power. Kissinger

examines the Congress of Vienna and European diplomacy
after Napoleon, focusing on Castlereagh, Talleyrand,
Metternich, and Alexander I. Assessing historical greatness
and anticipating his future superior and intellectual companion in the White House, Kissinger writes, "Those states-
men who have achieved final greatness did not do so
through resignation, however well founded. It was given to
them not only to maintain the perfection of order but to
have the strength to contemplate chaos, there to find ma-
terial for fresh creation."[2] Nixon loved to read deeply in
philosophy, theology, history, and biography. He especially
delighted in the intellectual perspectives diplomacy gives:
how human conflict is mediated, even transformed, to a
higher order by agile minds uniting idealism and pragmatism. Kissinger's visit would give me insight into whether
Nixon could mediate his own redemption from what Maurice
Blanchot called a self-destructive "foreign night," from a
world lost to Watergate, to a world restored in the self-re-
newing "passion of patience" and the discipline of writing.[3]

Nixon had deep affection and respect for Kissinger.
There is, of course, the famous account of Nixon asking
Kissinger to kneel down and pray with him near the Lincoln bedroom on August 7, 1974, the night before his resignation speech. Nixon pays Kissinger a high personal
tribute as recorded in his diary for Saturday, July 27, 1974.
It was three days after the U.S. Supreme Court had ordered
Nixon to turn over the tapes that would doom his presidency that Nixon realized resignation was inevitable. Nixon
wrote of Kissinger: "Henry came to see me, very mournful
but, bless him, he was thinking only with his heart. A very
unusual approach for a man who is so enormously endowed
with extraordinary intellectual capacity."[4]

Henry Kissinger's visit proved to be a watershed for my
assessment of Nixon's rehabilitation and my prescriptions

for his recovery. I recorded his blood pressure at a normal level of 140/90, a normal pulse rate of 74, and a normal sinus rhythm. These were all signs of his improving condition.

I decided that it was important for me to gain some insight into Nixon's attitude, so I purposely brought up certain political topics that we had not discussed in recent months, including Kissinger, President Ford and the pressures of inflation, West Germany and the Soviet Union, and the potential for war in the Middle East. Nixon spoke of Kissinger's brilliance and volatility. "Kissinger is a genius," Nixon began. "However, Henry is temperamental, very emotional, and most importantly must be guided. You use his tremendous ability and knowledge, but you have to make the decision and direct the policy. You can't let him run berserk," Nixon explained.

"Dick, how is President Ford doing with the economy?" I asked. Nixon's responses evolved into a complex discussion of politics and the economy in which he concluded that the major problem was inflation and that the danger of a recession was secondary.

"Jack, there are so many great pressures against Ford. I hope Ford has the stamina to withstand the liberal torrent to raise government spending," Nixon began.

"What if the president doesn't withstand the pressure?" I asked.

"If we have two years of a $50 billion deficit, inflation would become rampant," Nixon replied.

Nixon's prediction was accurate. While Ford did attempt a cosmetic "Whip Inflation Now" or "WIN" campaign, it never achieved real success. Jimmy Carter defeated Ford in the 1976 presidential election. Carter's increased spending coincided with the oil cartel's global embargo. Inflation and interest rates rose to record levels, nearly paralyzing the American economy and its influence in the world.

Next, I brought up foreign policy. "I have been impressed with the new West German chancellor, Helmut Schmidt, after seeing him on a television interview," I said. Nixon replied: "I have had discussions with Schmidt. He will be a tremendous statesman and hard-nosed diplomat, but he isn't the economist that Giscard d'Estaing is [the president of France in 1974]. If the Germans possessed an armed service worth anything, West Germany would be a real force in the balance of power struggle in Europe vis-a-vis the Soviet Union."

Nixon also expressed his concern that should there be war in the Middle East it would the "last gasping breath of Israel." Nixon understood the need to balance Egypt and Israel with a real peace, placate Jordan and protect Jordan's precarious position, resolve the Palestinian question, strengthen our alliance with Turkey, and deter the renegade terrorist states of Syria, Iran, and Iraq.

Nixon told me that he planned to leave La Casa Pacifica for the first time during his recovery and spend several days in February resting at the Annenberg estate in Palm Springs. We agreed that I would see him next on February 15. I asked Nixon whether I should respond to a request for an interview by Trudi Fellman, a reporter who was writing an article about Pat Nixon. He said that she had always been very fair in her reporting and that, if I wished, I should respond to her questions but not tell Pat that I had done this. Pat Nixon valued her privacy, and while her husband respected that desire, he also wanted the public to know about Pat's great virtues that had sustained him and his family. Nixon told me that his wife's inborn dignity, discipline, and loving influence during his tumultuous political career were what allowed him to handle and overcome intense periods of crisis.

14

Regimen for Recovery

ON THE AFTERNOON OF KISSINGER'S VISIT, I noted Nixon's immediate interest and renewed vigor in answering my questions, indicating that he was beginning to recover. In fact, my impression was that Nixon had shown the greatest amount of improvement in the shortest period of time since his serious illness began. Under these favorable conditions, I assessed that it was time to plan his future rehabilitation program.

"Dick," I began, "I feel it's time to outline your long-term recovery program." He answered: "Okay, Jack, let's have it." I replied, "My main priority is your health, both physical and mental. This means a gradual increase in your physical activities, such as more walking, perhaps putting, and eventually using La Casa Pacifica's three-hole golf course. Then, once you have gained more physical strength, I want you to begin playing regular rounds of golf at Camp Pendleton three to four days a week. Next, I want you to go out and appear more in informal public settings, such as small dinner parties and local restaurants, taking part in conversation with close friends and associates. From the mental aspect, I want you to begin to use your fine mind by writing. Remember, writing is the activity which you have always told me is the most physically and intellectually demanding exercise in the world." Nixon made a list of his New Year's resolutions for 1975:

Set great goals.
Daily rest.
Brief vacations.
Knowledge of all weaknesses.
Better use of time.
Write more books.
Golf or some kind of exercise everyday.
Articles and speeches on provocative new international and national issues.

In his first book, *Six Crises*, Nixon described writing the book as the "seventh crisis of my life, and by far the most difficult from the standpoint of the mental discipline involved." Nixon also referred to the mental and physical challenge of writing *Six Crises* and *In the Arena*, which he described as "ten months of the hardest work I had ever done."[1]

I knew it was imperative for Nixon to use his creative intellectual abilities and begin writing in order to fully recover. Nixon's mind was wide-ranging and deeply reflective. He hated small talk. Where others preferred camaraderie, he would rather read and reflect. "More pleasurable than TV, reading is also more efficient than talking. . . . Reading is active. It engages, exercises, and expands the mind," Nixon wrote in *In the Arena*.[2] Nixon also needed to express the ideas emerging from his inner reflection.

Although highly introspective, Nixon also needed to engage himself fully in public issues, in the realm of justice and the common good. In the introduction to *Six Crises*, Nixon described this innate desire: "A man who has never lost himself in a cause bigger than himself has missed one of life's mountaintop experiences. Only in losing himself does he find himself. Only then does he discover all the latent strengths he never knew he had and which otherwise would have remained dormant."[3]

I continued to see Nixon every three weeks at La Casa Pacifica, and I also received anticoagulation and blood pressure reports twice a week from Chief Dunn. Nixon's anticoagulation therapy remained at appropriate therapeutic levels. Nixon's resilient mental attitude ultimately allowed him to conquer his deep depression. In the weeks following my establishment of his rehabilitation regimen, Nixon affirmed his continued purpose in life in a letter to my youngest daughter, Elizabeth, then a high school student, who had sent him a birthday card in early January.

February 14, 1975
Dear Elizabeth:

I want you to know how very much your birthday
card meant to me, and particularly the handwritten
message which you enclosed with it.
I totally agree with your appraisal of your father.
He is an outstanding doctor, but even more important
a wonderful father and a loyal and good friend.
I only hope that as a result of the very fine medical
attention I have received from him and his colleagues
that I will be able to continue to work as a private
citizen for the cause of peace among all peoples to
which our Administration was so deeply dedicated.
    If, as a result of what we have done during the time
I served in the White House, young people like
yourself, wherever they might live in the world,
may grow up without experiencing the horrors of

war, it will have been all worthwhile, regardless of the rather rough experience we have had to endure in the recent past.

Mrs. Nixon joins me in sending our love and best wishes.

Sincerely,
Richard Nixon

Years later, on July 19, 1990, at the dedication of the Nixon Library, I reintroduced Elizabeth to Nixon during a recess in the dedication activities. "Dick, you remember Elizabeth," I said. Nixon replied without hesitation: "I surely do and particularly how deeply I appreciated her letter to me in the dark days of 1975 while she was still in high school."

In the spring of 1975, Nixon started receiving pressure from Watergate Special Prosecutor Henry Ruth to appear before a grand jury in Washington, D.C., on a Watergate-related matter. On May 27, in a letter to Ruth, I explained that such a trip still presented a risk to Nixon's health:

Based on my recent examination of the former President on the 23rd of May 1975, 1 have concluded that it would be physically possible for him to travel to Washington to appear before a grand jury. However, I have also concluded that travel to Washington and an appearance before a grand jury would create a more stressful situation than would exist if the former President were to provide his testimony at location near his home in California.

Although I can state without hesitation that the additional risk to the former President's health would exist were he to travel to Washington for a grand jury appearance, I am not in a position to quantify the degree of additional risk. There are a variety of factors which would work together to influence the amount of physical and emotional stress under those circumstances and no one but only God can predict with certainty the impact of those factors upon Mr. Nixon's health without him actually being subjected to them. I can only state, at this time, alternatives for obtaining Mr. Nixon's testimony not involving travel to Washington would pose a lesser degree of risk and therefore would be clearly preferable.

Ruth agreed to send the grand jury to San Clemente, where on June 1, 1975, in the old Western White House office compound, Nixon gave testimony for eleven hours.

Nixon made progress in his recovery over the summer and early fall. At this time, Nixon was fully engaged in writing his memoirs. Rose Mary Woods had rejoined the staff to assist on the book. On November 14, 1975, I went to La Casa Pacifica for a scheduled examination. Nixon told me that he was much more active physically and that the leg was fine. I was pleased, but I told him that Chief Dunn's reports indicated that prothrombine (clotting) time was too low and needed to be adjusted. I asked him about his normal routine and daily schedule. Nixon said that he read the paper in the morning and then went to his office at 9:30 A.M., where he stayed the rest of the day. He played golf on a regular basis every Monday and Friday. Nixon was now working eight-hour days. His stamina had returned.

While we were talking, Henry Kissinger called to discuss a potential opportunity to act as a consultant. Nixon was advising businesses on international trade and foreign policy issues to supplement his income. In this case, however, Nixon decided not to become involved in the endeavor discussed with Kissinger. Nixon detailed his difficult financial condition in memoirs: "I also had to recover my financial health. All my assets were invested in real estate. My Presidential and congressional pensions took care of ordinary expenses. But I had to find a way to pay up my attorney's fees. In addition, the government allowance for office expenses was inadequate to cover the staff I needed to answer my huge volume of mail. I needed extra income. I ruled out one potentially lucrative source, honoraria for speeches. It was not the right time for me to begin to speak out. But even more important, I had had a policy for not accepting honoraria for speeches ever since I had been elected Vice President in 1952."[4]

Accompanied by Secret Service agents, Nixon and I drove with Colonel Brennan to Camp Pendleton to play golf. During the trip to the golf course, we discussed my son Dan's intention to run for Congress for the seat once held by Craig Hosmer in Long Beach. Nixon said it might be well for Dan to come to San Clemente where he could give him some constructive political counsel. Nixon stressed that Dan should not get involved in the fight between the Reagan and Ford forces for the 1976 Republican presidential nomination. Nixon inquired about the district's demographics, its party percentages, and the strength of the incumbent. He told me to encourage Dan to run and said that if he felt strongly about certain controversial issues, such as abortion, he should honestly and firmly express his position but not belabor it. Dan ran for Congress in 1976 and lost by half a percentage point; he ran again in 1978 and spent ten years in Congress.[5]

Our golf game was enjoyable. Four Secret Service agents, each in a golf cart, accompanied us—two in front on either side of the fairway, called outriders, and two behind. A marshal went on ahead to direct golfers ahead who would then graciously let us go through. I noticed that the golfers and the public we encountered on the course were very friendly with Nixon, smiling and addressing him as "Mr. President."

Driving back to San Clemente, Nixon offered further suggestions about Dan's campaign, and we then spoke about Watergate and the press. "We will all have our day," he declared. "So much of this is based on a double standard. [Paul] Conrad's cartoon in the *Los Angeles Times* the other day showed Bebe Rebozo and me balancing a secret bank account in the Bahamas. Hell, I wish I did have a secret bank account. I sure could use the money. Also, the implication that Rebozo has a bank account other than his own is a damn lie.

"Let me give you another example," Nixon continued. "A newspaper recently published an article saying that my campaign manager in Illinois was indicted for fraud. Well, I had only met the son-of-a-bitch once. He was a defeated Republican state office candidate and the party had made him chairman of Citizens for Nixon. The alleged fraud activity had absolutely no connection at all with my campaign, yet the media reported it as such."

We arrived back at La Casa Pacifica, where we enjoyed a cocktail and agreed that I should return next time on a Friday so we could play golf again.

15

Dreadful Summoners

NIXON'S FINANCIALLY DIFFICULT SITUATION continued, even though he had received a large advance on his memoirs. His legal expenses were enormous, so out of necessity he agreed to do a series of televised interviews with the English journalist David Frost. Such major media undertakings demand underwriting by international insurers. The insurer indemnified the project investment and its successful conclusion, contingent on Nixon remaining healthy throughout the project.

On January 9, 1976, my son Brian drove me to La Casa Pacifica, primarily for my regularly scheduled visit to examine Nixon but also to meet Dr. Morey Blocker, medical director of the Fireman's Fund for the entertainment industry. Nixon and I met with Dr. Blocker in Nixon's office. Blocker was there to review Nixon's medical records, which I had brought with me.

During the journey to San Clemente, Brian expressed an interest in joining the Secret Service. I told Brian if that were the case then we would ask Nixon what he would advise. When I introduced Brian to Nixon, I told him of my son's interest in the Secret Service. Nixon said: "Brian, I know it appears to be a glamorous job, but it really is at times tedious and boring. I think that with your recent graduation from Notre Dame, you should be thinking of graduate study or another field of endeavor. However, if you wish, I will introduce you to the chief of my Secret Service detail." Brian reflected for a moment and said he appreciated the candor and the advice. He would follow his suggestion and explore other areas.[1]

After Brian had left the inner office, Nixon and I conferred privately before Dr. Blocker's arrival. I conducted a brief physical examination and asked him how he felt. Nixon responded, "Jack, I feel that I have improved immensely, physically and mentally, but financially I'm still in the wilderness."

"Why choose this clever and combative Englishman to conduct your first public interview after the resignation?" I asked.

"Jack, don't be so concerned. I have prepared many hours to handle Frost's tough—and what I know will be biased—questions. I am very aware of his aggressive technique and his focus on the sensational—true or not," Nixon replied. "My financial situation forces me to do this. My legal bills are enormous. I have to take care of this before I can really rebuild my life and dedicate my final years to helping achieve peace in the world," Nixon continued. (Nixon would earn $600,000 for the interviews; $540,000 was paid to his attorneys and $60,000 went to Swifty Lazar, his literary agent.)

We were informed of Dr. Blocker's arrival. Nixon and I greeted him as he entered. I told Dr. Blocker that he could look at Nixon's medical records, but that I would not give them to him because of the burglaries in 1972 during which they had been tampered with. I turned to Nixon and said, "You remember my office was broken into to get your records." Nixon replied humorously, "Yes, perhaps I had syphilis and that's why they wanted the records."

We reviewed Nixon's medical history, including the family trait of high blood pressure he had inherited, a condition that elevated under stress but, in my judgment, required no medication. Other than the nearly fatal phlebitis, Nixon said he had only been sick once in his life—the time he contracted brucelosis from the raw milk his father insisted that the family drink. Nixon told Blocker that he felt good, played golf three times a week, walked a mile and half a day, and swam for half an hour every night in the pool. I told Blocker that Nixon was on a regimen of anticoagulants and that his leg was normal except for being about 25 percent larger than the other leg. Dr. Blocker was satisfied; he thanked Nixon and me for our time and took his leave. As requested, I filed Nixon's medical report with the insurance brokers in July 1976.

The Frost interviews were taped in March 1977 and televised to a national audience entranced by the compelling one-on-one format. The Frost interviews were a substantive and dramatic success, as tens of millions of viewers watched all four broadcasts. The first interview was broadcast on the evening of May 4, 1977. The audience of 55 million viewers was the largest for a news interview in the history of television.

Once again in his public life, Nixon mesmerized the entire country and an international audience as he dueled Frost's rapier thrusts with a mixture of emotion, grandeur, self-pity, regret, defiance, and remorse. Nixon prepared himself well for the exhausting ordeal. Confident he could handle Frost, Nixon assumed King Lear's majestic bravado as the interviews commenced: "No, they cannot touch me for coining; I am the King himself."[2] Nixon ranged with eloquence and force on world politics—the Soviet Union, China, Vietnam—and domestic affairs. However, as Frost began to explore Nixon's mysterious role in the events of Watergate, he threw his clipboard to the floor almost as if he were foretelling the intense dramatic confrontation and purgation to follow.

Nixon was responding to Frost's challenge that it was imperative for him to admit to the American people more than mere "mistakes." Thus began a powerful and climactic exchange. "Well, what word would you express?" Nixon rejoined. Describing Nixon's query as "heart-stopping," Frost said the nation was waiting to hear him admit to wrongdoing, including an abuse of power, and offer an apology to the American people. Otherwise, Frost declared, "you're going to be haunted for the rest of your life."

Nixon was both remorseful and defiant. Nixon admitted to "horrendous" mistakes, "ones that were not worthy of a President . . . ones that did not meet the standards of excellence that I had always dreamed of as a young boy." For the first time, he spoke with remorse: "And for all those things, I have a very deep regret." However, Nixon then became defiant. "People didn't think it was enough to admit mistakes. Fine. If they want me to get down and grovel on the floor . . . No! Never! Because I don't believe I should," Nixon proclaimed.

You could see a catharsis beginning to take place. As Frost fired ever more direct and piercing questions, Nixon appeared shaken. The former president moved toward self-recognition, yet not without self-pity: "I brought myself down. I gave them a sword. And they stuck it in. And they twisted it with relish. And, I guess, if I'd been in their position, I'd have done the same." Protesting and admitting his guilt at the same time, Nixon reflected King Lear's famous lament:

Close pent-up guilts,
Rive your concealing continents and cry

These dreadful summoners grace. I am a man
More sinned against than sinning.[3]

Nixon went deeper into Watergate's infernal web. Frost implied that Nixon's involvement in tacitly approving hush-money payments to Watergate burglar E. Howard Hunt was part of an impeachable criminal conspiracy to cover up the break-in at Democratic National Headquarters. Defiant once more, Nixon denied that he had committed an impeachable offense because he "did not have the motive required for the commission of that crime." Asserting that he would have won an impeachment trial in the Senate by a narrow margin, Nixon abruptly reversed course and assigned to himself the ultimate responsibility for Watergate.

"I have impeached myself!" Nixon exclaimed. Unyielding, Frost retorted, "How do you mean, 'I have impeached myself'?"

"By resigning, that was a voluntary impeachment," Nixon conceded with increasing emotion, his eyes welling with tears.

Nixon plunged deeper still. Not waiting for Frost to propel him, he singled out his own conduct in protecting his aides. Nixon admitted that he had come to the very margins of legality, even crossing the threshold of criminal conduct. It was "in trying to protect Ehrlichman and Haldeman and all the rest as to how best to present their cases, because I thought they were legally innocent, that I came to the edge," Nixon declared. "And under the circumstances, I would have to say that a reasonable person could call this a cover-up," he confessed. Nixon's countenance now swelled with the deepest emotion: "I let down my friends. I let down the country. I let down our system of government and the dreams of all those young people that ought to get into government but think it's all too corrupt and the rest. . . . I let the American people down. And I have to carry that burden with me the rest of my life."

The interviews brought Nixon to a harrowing confrontation with himself, a self-encounter of unrehearsed intensity and confessional necessity:

> Something he left imperfect in the state,
> which since his coming forth is thought of, which
>   imports
> to the kingdom so much fear and danger that his
>   personal
> return was most required and necessary.[4]

16

Nixon in China

ON FEBRUARY 21, 1972, George Washington's birthday, it was very cold in Beijing. The airport was closed to all air traffic except for the arrival of the President of the United States. Dr. Li Zhisui, Mao Zedong's personal physician, observed the momentous meeting of Nixon and Mao from the entrance hall next to Mao's study. The "Red Flag limousine" pulled up with Nixon and Zhou Enlai inside. Nixon entered the residence first. Kissinger followed. According to Dr. Li Zhisui, Nixon was escorted so quickly into the residence that the Secret Service lost contact with him and did not know where he was. "One of the Chinese interpreters assured the American Secret Service that Nixon was safe with Mao," Dr. Li Zhisui explained.[1]

The reception hall where Mao initially greeted Nixon was built over Mao's large in-door swimming pool—no longer used because of his ill health. As Nixon entered the hall, he was immediately directed to Mao's study. Mao and Nixon approached each other with extended hands. Their hands met, and for two minutes their handshake continued, monumental and epochal.

After the meeting, pleased and enthusiastic, Mao removed his formal clothes, put his bathrobe on, and told

Dr. Li that Nixon was someone with whom he could deal and trust. "He speaks forthrightly—no beating around the bush, not like the leftists who say one thing and mean another," Dr. Li revealed. In light of this groundbreaking moment of diplomacy, it was only fitting that Nixon's first trip abroad since his resignation would be to China.

On February 20, 1976, the Chinese government sent a Boeing-727 to Los Angeles to fly Nixon and Pat to Beijing for a nine-day visit. Two medical corpsman and twelve Secret Service agents accompanied the Nixons. Nixon met with Chairman Mao and the senior Chinese leadership. He visited with Chinese factory workers in Canton, even trying to pedal a thresher at a tractor-assembly facility. Nixon could not operate the thresher alone, so a Chinese worker assisted him. Nixon said, "Ah—Chinese and Americans working together."[2]

Four days after his return, I drove to San Clemente to examine Nixon and received the first personal debriefing on the China trip. Kissinger had called two days earlier on behalf of President Ford and had asked for a written account. The *New York Times* reported that Kissinger apologized to Nixon for not coming in person.[3] Ford's advisers believed a personal visit by Nixon to China was politically embarrassing for Ford during an election year.

In our conversation, Nixon told me, "Except for Kissinger, Ford's people don't know how to handle the circumstances of my China trip. As a private citizen, I have the privilege of traveling to China or anywhere else I damn well please." He continued: "If my trip to China affects Ford in the New Hampshire primary so much, he ought to get the hell out of the race. By their attitude, you think I was talking to Chinese functionaries. They should be concerned about the national interest, not some half-assed primary. But don't kid yourself, Ford is damned anxious to find out what I know.

"The Chinese were very solicitous of my condition and sent the plane here for two reasons," Nixon continued. "The plane had two six-foot beds and two wardrobe closets for Pat and myself. They were concerned about my health and comfort. But the Chinese also wanted to accomplish a symbolic political gesture by landing a plane here with their flag on it," Nixon explained.

"I spoke with the Chinese leadership at length," Nixon said. "Since the death of Zhou Enlai [1976] there has been turmoil and a power struggle. Wua, the current leader, is just an interim figure. I don't think Mao will live much longer but some strong figure must take over—as of now, only dictatorships work in China. The Chinese still think of Mao as a god. He is eighty-eight years old; he's had one stroke; he has difficulty with his speech, and he drools some. But other than his speech problems, Mao's mental faculties are as acute as ever. Mao's speech problems frustrate him, as was the case with Eisenhower. Mao repeats through his interpreter or writes what he wants to say on a pad to the interpreter."

I asked Nixon if he had noted any great change in the four years since his historic visit in February 1972. "Jack," he said, "the Chinese people are basically more free to move about. One indication of more economic progress is they are wearing clothing with a greater variety of colors. I was able to meet the people this time. At Tianamen Square, Pat and I were nearly mobbed by the crowds. The same thing happened in Canton."

"Dick," I asked, "what about industrial progress?" Nixon replied:

China's fundamental problem is hunger, feeding nearly a billion people. The task before Chinese leaders is to introduce modern agricultural methods, but this will put a lot of people out of work. The new methods have to be introduced in a slower manner, but industrialization must increase faster to create jobs for those displaced in agriculture.

Listen, Jack, most Europeans and Americans don't realize it, but China is destined to become a world superpower by the year 2000. The simple fact is that there will be more than a billion Chinese by then, the world's largest consumer market and labor force. And what will ultimately make them a world leader is their makeup—they have a tremendous intelligence, drive, and desire to work.

"What is the Chinese view of Russia?" I asked. Nixon answered: "The Chinese have a mortal fear of Russia. The Chinese feel that there will ultimately be a war with Russia, just as happened with the Soviet Union's invasion of Czechoslovakia in 1968. Most Chinese want real friendship with the United States," Nixon continued. "They look at the U.S. as the only legitimate counterweight to Russia. But I don't think the American people consider this very important."

Nixon contrasted Chinese pride with American self-doubt and criticism:

I visited a commune and noticed how proud the Chinese were of their country, In America today, people are self-flagellating, criticizing everything and everybody. What they should do is go to another country and come back. Then they would be appreciative of America instead of criticizing the living daylights out of it. Media bears a lot of responsibility for this, as do our political leaders in the Congress. They investigate everything but themselves.

The commune I visited had seventy thousand people in it. They were so happy about their electrification and that each room had a twenty-watt bulb in it. The commune's director told me there were seventy televisions for the seventy thousand. This may or may not be a good idea. Television has had a negative effect on America for the past thirty years. Its great potential has been squandered. Media and broadcast executives bear a great responsibility for its misuse.

Nixon then discussed Chinese medicine: "I visited two hospitals and they were, unfortunately, pathetic. The equipment in the operating room reminded me of a dentist's chair. However, the Chinese have good medicine and good physicians. Acupuncture was not mentioned," Nixon informed me. "However, there was concentration on herbal medicine. Maybe the Chinese have something. You have to keep an open mind. Perhaps something startling will come out of Chinese medicine."

"You have to be wide open in science," I agreed. "Dr. John Lilly says that in order to conduct research on dolphins you must be open to the possibility that there are species on this earth just as intelligent as homo sapiens. But we are so high and mighty that we may someday find out that we are not the most intelligent—only the most wasteful of the gift of intelligence."

After Nixon's return from his personal fact-finding mission in China, he began to intensify his physical and mental activity. He played more golf, made more public appearances and foreign policy speeches. He resumed his voracious reading habits, concentrating on history, biography, philosophy, and theology; he began writing a series of books on leadership, foreign policy, and the future of America. Nixon was making remarkable progress in both his physical and intellectual goals. The trip to China not only helped Nixon's personal recovery but also inspired an opera celebrating his contribution to world diplomacy.

On October 22, 1987, the Houston Opera premiered *Nixon in China: An Opera in Three Acts* by John Adams; the libretto was by Alice Goodman. *Nixon in China* takes place during the six days of Nixon's visit to China in 1972. In addition to Nixon, the characters include Pat Nixon, Mao Zedong, Zhou Enlai, Madame Mao, and Henry Kissinger. Alex Ross, a music critic for the *New York Times*, believes that *Nixon in China* is one of the finest Americans operas, a powerful union of mythic characters, music, and words: "[*Nixon in China*] exhibits a more potent structure than nearly all its predecessors in the annals of American opera."[4] Ross expressed his concern that *Nixon in China* is not part of the standard operatic repertory in the great opera houses. He surmised that the reason is probably political. The opera has been produced less than six times since its Houston premiere, including the Brooklyn Academy of Music (1987), the John F. Kennedy Center for the Performing Arts (1988), and The Netherlands Opera (1988).

Alice Goodman's powerful libretto extends Nixon's visions of peace to succeeding generations. Invoking the ancient burial splendor of the Ming dynasty, Nixon uses Mao's own political rhetoric of "The Great Leap Forward" for the journey of youth to light:

> *Nixon:* Like the Ming Tombs. I think this leap
>   Forward to light is the first step
>   Of all our youth, all nations' youth
>   Our duty is to show them both

Their future and our past, the fire
And the noon glare.

17

Pat Nixon and The Final Days

MIKE WALLACE, THE CBS TELEVISION reporter who has covered most of the world's great personalities during the second half of the twentieth century, once told evangelist Billy Graham that of all the people he had ever met, he admired Pat Nixon the most.[1] Wallace's testimony is not surprising to those who knew Patricia Thelma Ryan Nixon. As her personal physician, I had the privilege of witnessing Pat Nixon's extraordinary, courageous conduct at close range, especially during ten years of physical illness and severe emotional distress from 1971 to 1980.

Four days after the nation's bicentennial on July 8, 1976, I admitted Pat Nixon to Memorial Hospital Medical Center with a diagnosis of cerebral hemorrhage and vascular hypertension—Pat Nixon had had a stroke. Her main complaints were of a generalized weakness of the left arm and leg, and a mild slurring of her speech. While in the swimming pool the previous afternoon, she had felt a strange weakness on her left side. I saw her in the hospital examining room and asked for more details so that I could further determine the severity of the stroke. The former First Lady

159

was a very private person, and it was difficult to obtain more information from her. Fortunately, Nixon and Julie Eisenhower were in the examining room. "Doctor," Julie related, "yesterday we noticed that during Mother's usual afternoon swim, she spent most of the time on the steps in the shallow end of the pool." "Pat appeared tired," Nixon added. "I saw her arise from her pool chair and slowly walk to her room." He continued, "I noticed Pat ate only a small portion of her dinner and her conversation was limited. A short time later she went to her bedroom. I asked Julie, 'Did you check your mother's room?'"

The following morning at 7:00, Pat Nixon was in the kitchen attempting to prepare her husband's coffee. Entering the room, Nixon noticed that his wife was having difficulty in performing this simple routine and that the left side of her mouth was lower than the right. Alarmed, Nixon immediately left the kitchen seeking Julie. When he found Julie, Nixon said, "Julie, I think your mother has had a stroke."

Nixon called me and explained his concern. I told him to call a physician from Camp Pendleton Marine Base. Shortly thereafter, the chief of medicine from Camp Pendleton arrived and examined Pat Nixon. After completing the examination, he told Nixon and Julie that she had suffered a small stroke and a significant elevation in blood pressure. He ordered immediate hospitalization, and an ambulance took Pat Nixon to Long Beach Memorial Hospital. I was waiting at the hospital. When she arrived, I concurred immediately with the diagnosis that she had suffered a stroke with marked restricted mobility on the left side of her body. In addition, her blood pressure was highly elevated. I gave my orders to the floor staff and then phoned Dr. Jack Mosher, an outstanding neurologist.

Following a consultation, we both informed Pat Nixon and her family of our diagnosis and prognosis for recovery. Outwardly, Pat Nixon responded to the diagnosis in her usual stoic fashion. However, after the family had left the room she whispered to me: "Jack, I am concerned not about myself but for the additional pressure my illness will have on Dick and the girls. You know that spinal needle was painful," she added, a rare concession to her own vulnerability. Nixon's reaction to the stroke was one of disbelief, then sorrow and visible tenderness. His daily visits to the hospital were marked by deep concern over her progress. Each morning when Nixon arrived, he would kiss her on the cheek and slip his hand into her left hand to give her comfort and check her grip for renewed strength.

Tricia Nixon arrived from New York late in the day. As I witnessed the tender love displayed by Tricia and Julie toward their mother, I perceived what a closely knit and loving family they were. I admired them for the way they responded to the horrifying trauma of Watergate, how they had stayed intact, how they had endured unimaginable shame, and how their love had prevailed and grown stronger. I remembered the famous picture taken by White House photographer Ollie Atkins in the upstairs living quarters of the White House on August 7, 1974, the day Nixon told his family he was going to resign: the family stands together smiling, linking arms and hands, bravely facing anguish—father, mother, two daughters and their husbands.

During Pat Nixon's fourteen-day hospital stay, the few visitors permitted included Jack and Helene Drown, Maureen Drown, Rose Mary Woods, and two members of the research team who were assisting Nixon with his memoirs, Frank Gannon and television anchorperson Diane Sawyer.

After the treatment for Pat Nixon's hypertension was successful, I began bedside physical therapy. As her condition improved, I ordered daily visits to the hospital's rehabilitation unit. Head nurse Connie Hamilton, who had cared for Nixon during his hospitalization two years earlier, monitored her progress. Pat Nixon's progress was remarkable. Her steadfast determination and desire to recover quickly to care for her husband and family accelerated her recovery. A few days before her discharge, Nixon came to see me and ask about his wife's prognosis.

"Jack, will Pat have continued physical therapy at home?" he asked.

"Yes, Dick," I replied, "we have arranged for a fine physical therapist to visit Pat daily. I am sure the home surroundings will greatly enhance her recovery—I have a gut feeling that she will make a complete recovery."

Suddenly, Nixon grabbed my right wrist, saying, "Jack, do you feel stress was a factor in the development of Pat's high blood pressure and stroke?"

"Yes, Dick," I said firmly.

"You know that two days before the stroke, Pat was reading *The Final Days*," Nixon revealed. Nixon's voice contained deep sadness and rising anger. "Pat was extremely upset over the sections where Woodward and Bernstein portrayed us as demented alcoholics and our marriage as loveless— pure, unadulterated lies!" Nixon exclaimed.

No human being can have greater access to a person's true inner thoughts, feelings, and character than priest or physician. Such deep understanding is all the more authentic when a physician cares for both husband and wife. Had Woodward and Bernstein asked me, I could have told them that their allegations would not have held up under scrutiny of the medical history of the Nixons, including my intimate knowledge of their health and conduct as their personal physician for more than a quarter of a century. If the Nixons had had a pattern of excessive drinking, I would have known it. None of the rigorous physical examinations and tests that I administered to the Nixons ever revealed any evidence of alcoholism, drug abuse, or physical violence. I also would have told them that, as I knew the Nixons, they had a deep and abiding love for each other that continued to grow despite the almost unbearable intensity of public life, which often drives spouses irretrievably apart. Nixon's very public and spontaneous expression of deep and passionate love at his wife's funeral in April 1993 would leave only the coldest heart unmoved.

The *New York Times* examined Woodward and Bernstein's journalistic method in an extensive essay by reporter Diedre Carmody, who identified several areas of professional and ethical concern: "What is raising questions is the fact that the book is written in a fiction-like style with no footnotes and relatively little attribution. It is sprinkled with direct quotations, and there are several descriptions of what people were thinking during critical moments. How were the authors able to reproduce verbatim quotes from conversations they had not heard? How did they know what the characters in their drama were thinking? And, since they do not trace the sources of their information, why should the reader believe them?"[2]

Mike Wallace acknowledges Pat's praiseworthy character, and David Halberstam believes that she is one of the great heroines of American public life. Halberstam admires her from the perspective of human values and sympathy for a great person. Two weeks after her death in April 1993, Halberstam was interviewed by Brian Lamb about his book *The Fifties* on the C-Span program *Booknotes*. Lamb asked

Halberstam to assess Pat Nixon, about whom Halberstam had written in *The Fifties*.

Halberstam gives Pat Nixon her due. "Pat Nixon. I think she's heartbreaking," explains Halberstam with obvious and heartfelt empathy. "She has a childhood so harsh it is Dickensian. It is hard as if she lived in the time of Charles Dickens. It's hard to imagine anyone with so difficult a life. Her mother, who's the one person she really loves, dies when she's young. Her father dies. She raises her brothers, cooks for them, keeps house, cleans, and then goes off and studies herself, puts herself through school. Utterly admirable, really beautiful when she was young, eventually marries Richard Nixon."[3]

There was a prevailing but inaccurate view about Pat Nixon that was propagated by many members of the press corps: that she was the stereotypical, compliant American wife of the 1950s, slavishly following her husband through career and heartbreak. Even in this context, Pat Nixon continues to mesmerize Halberstam, although I believe he succumbs to the prevailing myth of passivity. Asked by Lamb how he accounts for Nixon's very emotional reaction at her funeral: "Maybe it finally came home to him how much she had given him and how high a price she had paid. She's really fascinating. She's a classic wife of the fifties—stoic, do what your husband wants even if it's not what you do, go along with it, that's your role."[4]

In a predominating myth, there is another caricature of Pat Nixon—that she was the unquestioning, passive, silent partner, listening, adoring, obedient to her husband, hating politics and remaining aloof from it. On the contrary, Pat Nixon was very actively involved in politics and her husband's career, reading every morning, for example, the editorial pages of newspapers such as the *Wall Street Jour-*

nal well before her husband had even read the sports pages. I believe President Ronald Reagan's private letter of condolence to Nixon on his wife's death expressed most eloquently the true essence of Pat Nixon. Handwritten in his famous vertical cursive, Reagan wrote:

> June 22, 1993
> Dear Dick:
>
> After we spoke to you this morning to convey our sympathies on Pat's passing, Nancy and I sat together and reflected on Pat's wonderful life. From serving as a model "political partner," by distinguishing herself in her own right as our nation's First Lady, Pat made this world a better place. Throughout her time in public life she embodied the goals and aspirations of women across the land.
>
> As you took the many historic steps of your Presidency that made this world a safer place, Pat was always there gracefully at your side. And at those difficult times when your political fortunes were down, Pat was proudly there to help you overcome the challenges and tribulations.
>
> Nancy and I fondly remember the many happy times we spent with you both. And like the rest of America, we will greatly miss her.
>
> Our deepest sympathies go out to you and your family.
>
> Sincerely,
> Ron

18

New Glory

FATE'S WHEEL OF FIRE brought Richard Nixon to the far radius of human anguish and exile. Andre Malraux wrote to Whittaker Chambers after reading *Witness,* Chambers's classic autobiography of a soul in conflict: "You are one of those who did not return from Hell with empty hands."[1]

Neither did Richard Nixon.

The former president's life is the biography of a soul in spiritual and moral conflict emancipating itself. Nixon never yields—though severely tempted and pushed—to the dark, destructive forces of alienation and despair. It is as if Nixon had a primal understanding of what he had to do to climb out of hell. At the end of the *Inferno,* Dante plots his own escape and liberation with his moral guide, Virgil; but it is his love for Beatrice that inspires his recovery from the brink of death. In Richard Nixon's struggle toward redemption, his beloved Pat would prove to be both his Virgil and his Beatrice.

In October 1974, I witnessed Nixon's seventh and final crisis deepen into the catharsis of a spirit in exile. During the intimate dinner Lorain and I shared with the Nixons, Nixon surprised himself by asking us a rhetorical question that invited inner dialogue with conscience: What had he done wrong? With this question, Nixon had initiated his own climb out of hell. This arduous ascent culminated in a full contrition before the world in 1977, when David Frost's powerful interview impelled Nixon to admit guilt, express remorse, and apologize.

On those two critical occasions, Nixon confronted and acknowledged his own human fallibility and the anguish it caused. It is in this context that I have recounted his illness and recovery: as a narrative of anguish and redemption. In the personal torment of Watergate—resignation, grave illness, and exile—Nixon learned much about anguish and redemption. He learned what Sophocles understood about human anguish: "The greatest griefs are those we cause ourselves."[2] Nixon's ordeal taught him what Shakespeare admonished about the preconditions for redemption: "Bear free and patient thoughts."[3] Yet Nixon did not stop at self-awareness. He learned the peace that binds compassion to commonwealth in experiencing the anguish of expatriation and exile from his home in San Clemente.

The more I practiced medicine, the more I marveled at the profound relationship between the body and the mind. The unity between mind and body affects every human being as a mysterious union of immense and final consequence. I developed the conviction that the mental attitude of a patient plays a decisive role in the onset of many diseases, in the response to the treatment, and certainly in the mind-set of a patient who announces that death is imminent.

I witnessed Richard Nixon's recovery from the deepest devastation, the "black whirlwind," to normality. I treated and observed him during great mental and physical anguish as well as when he restored his life from the wreckage of Watergate. I saw him at the edge of death, in dark depression, and later witnessed the reemergence of his will to live.

I knew most acutely how the ordeal of Watergate, the resignation of the presidency, and the near-fatal illness had weighed upon Nixon's mind. I knew that unless Nixon actively pursued constructive engagement with himself and the external world, despondency and despair would triumph. Nixon had to resist the oncoming threat of annihilation. "From the moment when the imminent silence of the immemorial disaster caused him anonymous and bereft of self, to become lost in that other night . . . from that moment on, the passion of patience . . . had to be his sole identity," writes Maurice Blanchot.[4]

In January 1975, as recounted earlier, I charted for Nixon a regimen of rehabilitation and self-reconstruction, including physical, social, and intellectual exercise. I directed Nixon to swim and play golf, initiate and accept social engagements with close friends, and begin actively using his mind by writing. Nixon revealed a normal resistance to negative onslaughts. It is my professional judgment that Nixon was within the normal range of controlled mental and physical reactions of anger, love, elation, sorrow, humility, compassion, and resentment. This basic range of human feeling was always accompanied by a deep desire for a peaceful world. I observed many of my patients regain health and well-being from grave illnesses during the more than forty-five years I practiced medicine. However, never did I witness such a remarkable will to live and desire to participate in life as I did with my patient Richard Nixon.

At the end of his life, Winston Churchill fell into a dark despondency from which he could not extricate himself. When Churchill resigned as prime minister and retired from public life amid universal acclaim in 1955, he told his personal physician, Sir Charles Wilson (Lord Moran), "I'm waiting for death. But it won't come."[5] Lord Moran explains in the preface to his diaries why he refused to write about the last five years of Churchill's life:

> When, however, Winston ceased to count in politics, when in a sense he could no longer be said to be responsible, I began to question whether there was any purpose in preserving a chronicle of his failing powers. During the last five years of his life I continued from habit to make notes in my casebook, but apart from the two alarming accidents when he broke his spine and fractured his femur, the short entries in my diary add little to the record. I have thought it proper to omit the painful details of apathy and indifference into which he sank after his resignation, because they are no longer of historical significance, and so I bring my story to an end five years before his death.[6]

Nixon, however, never yielded to despair as Churchill did in the twilight of his career. Although Nixon personified the most ignominious disgrace to much of the world when he resigned the presidency in 1974, he refused to let the horrific shame and humiliation destroy him. I was continually amazed by Nixon's remarkable ability to withstand the most devastating experience with a resilient courage. While Churchill could not contend with loss of power and increasing physical debilitation, Nixon overcame the most shameful abdication of power conceivable, a nearly fatal illness, and profound psychological anguish. Churchill descended into a deep melancholy never to return, never again to use the majesty of the English language in writing or speech.

Nixon's ability to achieve redemption was evident in the profound concern for world peace that characterized his life. In June 1974, despite the intense pressure of Watergate and his painfully swollen left leg, Nixon traveled to Egypt to meet President Sadat and craft a peace in the Middle East. The trust and solidarity between Nixon and President Sadat set in motion a structure for peace that would result in Sadat's breathtaking speech to Israel's Knesset in 1977 and the Camp David Accords under President Carter in 1979.

Yet tragic days lay ahead for the two leaders who had such an affinity for each other. Nixon would resign within two months, and Sadat would be assassinated in the fall of 1981.

Nixon admired Sadat greatly for his boldness and vision. Nixon expressed this in his toast at the state dinner in Cairo on June 12, 1974. In describing Sadat's leadership, Nixon said that true leaders of nations do not neglect domestic or international affairs but recognize that they are "inseparable." Nixon believed that Sadat manifested this quality in historic terms, earning the respect of not only friends but adversaries.

During the news conference, Sadat was asked what was the primary contribution the United States could make for a sustained peace in the Middle East. In a remarkable response, Sadat argued that it was the trust and faithfulness inspired by Nixon that was the guarantor of peace in the region. Sadat explained that his people's reception of Nixon had confirmed the trust that Nixon inspired in the international sphere. "And President Nixon," Sadat concluded, "never gave a word and didn't fulfill it; he fulfilled every word he gave."[7]

The tragic irony is that just as Nixon's mastery of trust between nations ascended—creating structures of peace—

Watergate was destroying every political and moral sinew of trust Nixon had with the American people.

In October 1971, President Nixon invited my wife and me to a state dinner at the White House in honor of Josef Broz Tito, president of Yugoslavia. Twenty-five years later, the United States and Europe would be contending with Tito's doomed legacy in the Balkans. Yugoslavia was an artificial state, a divisive amalgamation of ethnicities and religions coerced and intimidated into nationhood. In the receiving line at the state dinner, President Tito was dressed in black-tie attire and his wife in a beautiful evening dress. As my wife and I edged closer, I noticed that Tito appeared to be uncomfortable and uneasy in the tuxedo and black tie; he looked as if he preferred a military uniform. As I shook hands with Tito, I recalled Lord Moran's diary entry of more than a quarter century earlier regarding Tito in Naples at a luncheon for Allied commanders. Tito is followed everywhere by two bodyguards "bulging with pistols" and looking like they belong in a Victor Herbert musical as "Ruritarian" palace guards.[8]

When Tito died, he left no mediating institutions, only a political vacuum, which was filled by arms, terror, and genocide. The genocidal killings in Bosnia, Serbia, and surrounding Balkan states since Yugoslavia's break-up reveal the tragic irresolution of the West and its selective morality in permitting the mass murder of hundreds of thousands of Muslims since 1991.

Nixon condemned the equivocation of the United States and Europe over the Balkan genocide in *Beyond Peace*. Nixon argued that in 1991 the United Nations should have lifted arms embargo against Bosnia to restore the balance of power and allow the Bosnians to defend themselves against the Serbians. The United Nations did not, and the result was horrific—massacres on a genocidal scale.

Nixon severely criticized the failure of the United States to act in Bosnia, a failure that has destroyed America's stature as an "evenhanded player" in international diplomacy, especially with the Islamic world. Nixon referred to Samuel P. Huntington's now-famous 1996 *Foreign Affairs* article warning against a "clash of civilizations" manifested in a potentially dangerous impasse and confrontation between Islam and the West. Nixon admonished: "The United States must not let the 'clash of civilizations' become the dominant characteristic of the post–Cold War era. As Huntington observed, the real danger is not that this clash is inevitable but that by our inaction we will make it a self-fulfilling prophecy. If we continue to ignore conflicts in which Muslim nations are victims, we will invite a clash between the Western and Muslim worlds."[9]

Moreover, Nixon observed, America and the West must take their responsibilities to an even higher level than merely avoiding conflict, to a level beyond peace—to the kind of harmonious vision and understanding between religions and cultures that Pope John Paul II called for in his encyclical *Ut Unum Sint* (That They May Be One): "What is needed is a calm, clear-sighted and truthful vision of things, a vision enlivened by divine mercy and capable of freeing people's minds and inspiring in everyone a renewed willingness."[10]

In two extraordinary paragraphs in *Beyond Peace,* paragraphs concluding the chapter entitled "Building Bridges to the Muslim World," Nixon contends that strength and power—while prerequisites—are not sufficient for America's ultimate role in the world. It is rather "great ideas," both religious and secular, that can truly fulfill America's destiny. Islam and the West cannot only cooperate on social, economic, and political levels but can also share each other's insights into the eternal: "The twentieth century has been a period of conflict between the West and the Muslim world. If we work together we can make the twenty-first century not just a time of peace in the Middle East and the Persian Gulf, but a century in which beyond peace, two great civilizations will enrich each other and the rest of the world—not just by their arms and their wealth but by the eternal appeal of their ideals."[11]

Nixon's vision here has gone beyond his incisive and compelling five-power or pentagonal balance-of-power equation for the post–Cold War world. As early as 1971, Nixon perceived the waning of the Cold War alliances and antagonisms into pentagonal arrangement—the United States, Europe, Japan, China, and Russia—according to James Chace and Nicholas Rizopoulos writing in *World Policy Journal*. In 1972, Nixon "articulated a concept of a new concert of great powers."[12]

Former Secretary of State Madeline Albright has often declared that the United States remains the indispensable nation to ensure conditions of equity and fairness for global development. Richard Nixon has always observed that the United States must lead being the world's preeminent military and economic power. For Nixon, there is one ultimate question of the new millennium: Will the United States be *worthy* of its great historical assignment and challenge?

"Are we worthy to lead?" Nixon inquires, and he answers that "we cannot unless we project values that go beyond peace, beyond our security, beyond our wealth."[13] The United States must embody in both principle and action those virtues of sacrifice, faithfulness, discipline, integrity, generosity, dedication, sympathy, constancy, and love that invest freedom with eternal value and significance.

Nixon begins his author's note at the end of *Beyond Peace* by observing that it is "my tenth book, and my ninth since resigning the presidency twenty years ago this year." A prolific author, he spent countless hours devoting his talents to the greater good. Nixon wrote *Beyond Peace* not just for East and West but for all of humanity, including Muslims and Christians and Jews, Hindus and Buddhists, agnostics and atheists, rich nations and poor nations, immigrants and natives, ideologues and pragmatists, young and old.

It was almost as if in his author's note Nixon had brought us both back to that bright fall day in Pomona when he and I first met. There amid golden groves of orange and lemon trees we began that whistle-stop railway tour through California's Great Central Valley and were carried into history by the engines of Santa Fe El Capitan under the broad summits of the San Gabriel Mountains. I understand now that Richard Nixon was telling me in his "real heart" that this was his great enterprise, his great historic task—to demonstrate by his life, as Thoreau phrased it, that "we . . . have discovered only the shores of America" and that we must explore "the interior beyond the shores of America . . . to meet the expectation of the land."[14]

La Casa Pacifica could easily have become Napoleon's Black Room on St. Helena, the emperor's quarters on the austere Atlantic island to which Napoleon was banished in 1815 after his defeat at Waterloo. In the Black Room, Napoleon lived in vain retrospection of his fallen greatness. Until his death in 1821, Napoleon would conduct endless empty conversations reprising past glory by himself or with his retinue. Nixon too could have yielded to the temptation of melancholy, ennui, and ever-repeating nostalgia. At La Casa Pacifica, however, Nixon defied despair. On St. Helena, Napoleon was vainglorious. "If truth conflicts with his glory he chooses glory," writes Jean-Paul Kaufmann.[15] Nixon would overcome vainglory and choose veracity.

When Nixon moved to New Jersey in the early 1980s, I transferred his medical care to physicians in New York because of logistics and distance. However, Nixon and I continued our conversations and political dialogue by correspondence. In 1991, Nixon sent me a wistful letter reminiscing about our friendship and my medical care, the ordeal of Watergate, his illness, and the "Lungren political tradition" (my son Dan was elected attorney general of California in November 1990).

> April 16, 1991
> Dear Jack,
>
> I could hardly believe it when I heard that
> young doctor who traveled with me in the
> 1952, 1956 and 1960 campaigns and who saw
> me through a tough ordeal in 1974 is shortly
> going to celebrate his 75th birthday.
>   Since you were always such a much better
> golfer than I was, I assumed you were about
> ten years younger. Now, like me, you can look
> forward to the time when you will say that life
> begins at 80!
>   Pat and I will always be grateful for the wise
> counsel and friendship Lorraine [*sic*] and you
> have extended to us over the years. And we
> are as please [*sic*] as I'm sure both of you are
> that Danny is carrying on the Lungren
> political tradition in such brilliant fashion.
>
> With warm regards,
> Sincerely,
> Dick

On April 18, 1994, Nixon suffered a stroke at his home in New Jersey. He was taken to New York Hospital–Cornell

Medical Center where he was placed in intensive care. The hospital issued a statement that he was "out of grave danger," stable with "partial paralysis on his right side and unable to speak," and "alert, in good spirits and able to understand."[16] The statement noted that Nixon would be moved out of the intensive care unit to a private room, but it was "uncertain" whether his neurological condition would improve.

Richard Milhous Nixon died on Friday, April 22, 1994, at 9:08 A.M., of complications from the stroke suffered four days before. Nixon was eighty-one years old. I immediately made plans to attend the funeral with my family. Nixon's funeral was held on April 27, 1994, at the Richard Nixon Library and Birthplace in Yorba Linda, California. President Clinton and former presidents Bush, Reagan, Ford, and Carter attended with their wives. Eulogies were given by former Secretary of State Henry Kissinger, Senate Majority Leader Robert Dole, California Governor Pete Wilson, President Clinton, and Rev. Billy Graham. Attending the funeral was an extraordinary assemblage of both elite and grassroots politicians, friends, former adversaries, ambassadors, foreign dignitaries, and national and international media. More than two thousand guests and envoys from forty-seven countries, five presidents, and more than a hundred Senate and House members attended the funeral.

Even Nixon's antagonists in song had lowered their polemics as if to proclaim as Shakespeare in *King Lear.* "Vex not his ghost: O, let him pass!"[17] This solicitude was exercised in honor of the way Nixon conducted his life after Watergate had nearly ended it. Neil Young had written a song in the early 1970s called "Ohio," which blamed Nixon for the killing of four students at Kent State by the National Guard during a campus protest against Nixon's incursion into Cambodia in the Vietnam War:

Tin soldiers and Nixon coming.
This summer I hear the drumming,
Four dead in Ohio.

By the time of Nixon's death, however, Neil Young had written another song, "Campaigner," more bittersweet and forgiving than condemning, with each stanza ending in the plaintive refrain:

Where even Richard Nixon has got soul,
Even Richard Nixon has got it, Soul.

At Nixon's death, his closest compatriots and colleagues expressed a deep, personal grief. In his funeral eulogy, Henry Kissinger said that when "I learned the final news, by then so expected, yet so hard to accept, I felt a profound void."[18] Senator Robert Dole spoke in a trembling voice, tears in his eyes: "I believe the second half of the twentieth century will be called the 'age of Nixon.' Why was he the most durable public figure of our time? Not because he won every battle, but because he embodied the deepest feelings of the people he led."[19] California Governor Pete Wilson stated that "it's hard to imagine a world without Richard Nixon. For half a century he played a leading role in shaping the events that have shaped our lives. . . . because his intellect, his insight, and his indomitable will could not be ignored."[20] President Clinton spoke of Nixon's tenacious enthusiasm for life: "But the enduring lesson of Richard Nixon is that he never gave up being part of the action and passion of his time." In further tribute to Nixon's life, President Clinton continued, "May the day of judging President Nixon on anything less than his entire life and career come to a close."[21] On April 24, Bob Schieffer, CBS News chief Washington correspondent, offered a pungent yet poignant assessment of Nixon on *Face the Nation*: "Richard Nixon left the White House in disgrace, but he left the earth with dignity."

Richard Nixon's resignation of the presidency and the personal and public devastation wrought by Watergate to himself, his family, and the nation possess the tragic dimension of King Lear dividing and surrendering his kingdom. Maureen Dowd of the *New York Times* covered Nixon's funeral and found allusions to Shakespeare in the tempestlike weather conditions, the comments of observers at the funeral, and her own thoughts.

> In a scene worthy of *King Lear*, the usually sunny California sky unleashed thunder, lightning, rain and hail today as Richard M. Nixon's body returned to its birthplace in a plain wooden coffin covered by a flag.
>
> Mr. Nixon brought forth Shakespearean references from both admirers and detractors in the crowd today. Mike Yoder of Fullerton said, "I kept thinking about *Hamlet*: 'Take him for all he's worth. He was a man. We shall never see his like again.' That's a paraphrase, that's not exact but that's what I keep thinking about Nixon."
>
> As the once exiled leader's daughters brought him to his burial place, the storm began howling and raging recalling the scene in *King Lear* when one of Lear's daughters turns the King out into the storm with the admonition: "To willful men, the injuries that they themselves procure must be their schoolmasters." Many in the crowd seemed flabbergasted at the freakish tempest. When the hail began falling, a member of the group of Chinese mourners commented: "When a great man dies, there are always storms."[22]

While the hail and winds may have raged at Yorba Linda, Nixon had at last subdued his inner storms and purged, as Denise Levertov wrote, the "familiar imagination of disaster."[23]

> A cadence of peace might balance its weight
> on that different fulcrum; peace, a presence,
> an energy field more intense than war,
> might pulse then,
> stanza by stanza into the world,
> each act of living
> one of its words, each word
> a vibration of light . . .[24]

The last honor guard ended martial stride, and the Navy bugler blew the final plaintive note of taps. Navy jets in the missing man formation roared overhead in salute, then curved away disappearing into storm clouds. A mysterious silence fell over the crowd of mourners.

At that moment, Colonel Brennan came over to me. Tears were in his eyes. Brennan put his arm around my shoulders and said, "Doctor, thank you for giving 'The Boss' twenty more years of life in which he was able to redeem himself." Brennan could say no more, and neither could I. The plangent, slate-gray clouds roiled above us. Strangely, the swelling turbulence produced no rain.

Unsettled, I thought of the lemon trees that Nixon's father had planted in Yorba Linda, a grove of trees next to the home Frank Nixon built from a catalogue kit for his family and from which Hannah Nixon picked the bittersweet fruit for her beloved son Richard and his brothers. In Yorba Linda, the lemon trees no longer exist, but their memory remains as "trumpets of gold," portending salvation.[25]

In his farewell speech, given on an overcast, fateful Friday morning, August 9, 1974, when Richard Nixon left the White House for the last time as president of the United States, he spoke of his deepest roots, of his father, "a great man," and his mother, "a saint," and of the lemon grove—"the poorest lemon ranch in California." And then, near the end, Nixon spoke of the light seemingly lost forever to Teddy Roosevelt when his beloved young wife died. Now, in his own deepest travail, Richard Nixon affirmed that such redeeming radiance never goes out, is never extinguished: "We think, as T.R. said, that the light had left his life forever. Not true. It is only a beginning, always. The young must know it; the old must know it. It must always sustain us."[26]

Banished between two great geophysical upheavals, the East Pacific Rise and San Andreas Fault, at San Clemente, California, Nixon would seize that intrepid inner light and reconstruct his life, restoring his name and redeeming his honor. While caring for Nixon's crisis of body I witnessed his crisis of soul, the deep moral ordeal and upheaval that returned him to "the fidelity of things,"[27] conscience and honor. This drama of salvation now was concluded. I had fulfilled my profound charge and duty. I had returned Richard Nixon, the resigned president of the United States, to the American republic—whole and intact. Richard Milhous Nixon chose not to look back from his exile but to engage life and reoccupy its commodious rooms.

Appendix

Nixon's Six Crises

Richard Nixon wrote *Six Crises* in 1961, after his narrow defeat by John F. Kennedy in 1960 and just before he agreed to run for governor of California in 1962. Nixon selected six singular events in his early career that significantly influenced him as a political leader and a future president.

Crisis 1: The Alger Hiss Case

The Hiss Case concerns the alleged espionage for the Soviet Union by a high level state department official, Alger Hiss, and his accuser, Whittaker Chambers, a former friend of Hiss and a senior editor at *Time Magazine.* Chambers had been a member of a communist apparatus whose purpose was to infiltrate senior government offices and steal secret documents. A reluctant witness, the shy and disheveled Chambers accused the suave and handsome Hiss of espionage. Hiss denied the charges.

Despite Hiss's apparent credibility, Chambers would not be abandoned by Nixon, and he eventually linked Hiss to espionage using the famed "Pumpkin Papers," a cache of secret microfilm kept on his Maryland farm. Hiss was later convicted of perjury and sentenced to prison.

Crisis 2: The Fund

The 1952 election campaign presented Senator Nixon with a personal crisis that almost drove him off the Republican ticket with Eisenhower. On September 14, 1952, a reporter asked Nixon about a "secret fund" of between $18,000 and $20,000. Nixon did have such a fund, but it was not a secret. It only was used for office expenses and official travel. The fund story soon went national, alleging that Nixon had misappropriated $16,000 for personal use. A headline in the *Washington Post* declared: "Secret Rich Man's Trust Fund Keeps Nixon in Style Far Beyond His Salary." Both the *Washington Post* and *New York Herald Tribune* called for his resignation.

Nixon decided to answer the charges on national television. He forcefully refuted the allegations with a thirty-minute discussion of his personal and political finances, a presentation that generated overwhelming support by the American people. Near the end of his address, Nixon said that he would not return one gift—a dog, Checkers, given to his two daughters.

Crisis 3: The Heart Attack

Nixon received the news of Eisenhower's heart attack on Saturday, September 25, 1955. Eisenhower was at the summer White House in Denver when he suffered a mild coronary. Nixon was thrust into the limelight as the immediate successor to the president, forced to walk a balance between governing the nation and not appearing conspicuous. The looming reelection campaign made Nixon's leadership all the more sensitive.

Nixon performed well, and within two months Eisenhower was able to resume the complete duties of his office.

Crisis 4: Caracas

In 1958, Vice President Nixon and his wife made a trip to eight Latin American countries to assess their social and political situations. Incidents in two countries put Nixon in physical danger. The first was in Lima, Peru, where communist organizers and students demonstrated, screaming "Muera Nixon! Death to Nixon!" and throwing rocks, one of which grazed the Vice President's shoulder. Nixon's motorcade was able to leave quickly, whisking him away to safety, and he later spoke to students at the nearby Catholic university.

Caracas, Venezuela, presented a serious threat of assassination, yet Nixon decided to visit the country as scheduled. In Caracas, an even more dangerous crowd surrounded the Nixon motorcade, which now included Pat Nixon and a Secret Service protection contingent. The demonstrators turned violent, hurling rocks and bottles at the limousine and rocking it to turn it over. The Secret Service extricated Nixon and his wife from the riot and transported them to safety. The Nixons received a hero's welcome when they returned to America.

Crisis 5: Khrushchev

In July 1959 Nixon traveled to Moscow, where he had an extraordinary meeting with Soviet Premiere Nikita Khrushchev that culminated in the famous "kitchen cabinet" debate on worldwide television. The debate was a one-on-one confrontation in which the earthy Khrushchev tried to put Nixon off balance during a conversation they were having in front of an American kitchen exhibit at a trade conference. Nixon handled the challenge with crisp, substantive responses to the Soviet leader. Again, Nixon received the admiration and support of the American people when he returned home.

Crisis 6: The Campaign of 1960

The 1960 presidential campaign was probably the most interesting in recent American history: Two evenly matched opponents, Kennedy and Nixon, competed for the support of the American public in four closely fought television debates. Eight thousand votes mysteriously appeared in Chicago and swung the Illinois electorate in Kennedy's favor. He won the presidency, and Nixon declined to challenge the election results.

The Burglaries at My Medical Office

Nixon was especially sensitive to the privacy and security of his medical records. On two occasions in September 1972, my medical office in Long Beach was burglarized. In both instances, the steel walk-in safe was forced open. It contained accounts receivable, small change, and Nixon's medical records from his legislative and vice-presidential tenure. On the second invasion of my office on September 21, I reported the incident to the Long Beach police. It was apparent to me that the major objective for the break-in was to obtain the Nixon file and have its contents photographed.

Before the arrival of the local police and the FBI, I had the Memorial Hospital photographers photograph the scene without touching or moving the disarray of Nixon's medical records on the floor. I was questioned by both the local police and the FBI agents. At that particular period in time, I had no further communications with either the police or the FBI. The national media, I might add, remained silent about the event.

On Friday, May 4, 1973, a six-inch headline announced the story in the *Long Beach Independent Press-Telegram*: "Nixon Medical Files Rifled Here in 1972." The entire episode was recounted, but the article received second billing. The evening edition front page headline was a story concerning a police car crash killing two people; the other feature was entitled "White House Half Crucified Me . . . Martha Said, Pat Joins in GOP Tactics." This was accompanied with a large picture of Martha Mitchell carrying a bible. On page six, the headline read: "Nixon Warns Hanoi as an Aggressor." This was placed next to a picture of President Nixon with his friend Bebe Reboza, which was unrelated to the lead article.

The burglary of my office was only reported by the local paper and was ignored by the big eight of "objective" journalism; the *New York Times*, the *Washington Post*, the *Los Angeles Times*, *Newsweek*, *Time*, CBS, NBC, and ABC had no immediate reporting of the incident. It defies logic that a break-in at the office of the personal physician of the president of the United States and the probable copying of his medical records was not reported by any national newspaper or television news organization for seven months.

In an affidavit given October 1973 to the FBI, I noted: "I examined the president's records in this file folder and found them to be out of chronological order in which they were maintained. This led me to speculate that the president's records had been examined and, perhaps, photographed, although I am aware of nothing of a compromising or embarrassing nature contained in those records." Apparently the burglars found nothing useful, for the issue of Nixon's health did not arise during the remainder of his presidency until the very end.

Excerpt from the Press Conference on October 27, 1974

In Dr. Lungren's statement to the press (p.102), he also acknowledged by name the persons and institutions that had provided assistance in the treatment of Nixon: "The physicians included doctors Wiley Barker, Donald Mulder, Seibert Pearson, Eldon Hickman, Scott Driscoll, James Harper, James Patton, Melvin Campbell, Al Jennings, Richard Henke, James Baker, Eunice Larson, John Anderson, Earl Dore, Dennis Mc Quown, and myself—all board-certified in their particular fields. In addition, we had the valuable help and direction of the following men from the department of pharmacy of Memorial Hospital Medical Center and the Medical College of Virginia: Dr. William Smith, Dr. William Barr, Dr. Dennis Mackewicz, and Dr. Larry Cacace. Finally, we had the total and complete devotion of the members of the nursing service at Memorial Medical Center."

Nixon and the Entertainment Industry

Nixon once appeared on *Laugh In,* a popular television series produced by Paul Keyes, in a ridiculous cameo. Nixon looked at the camera and yelled, "Sock it to me?"

There was the famous visit of Elvis Presley to meet Nixon at the White House in 1970, now memorialized and commercialized by a book, tee shirts, and coffee mugs. Elvis gave Nixon a pistol and asked him if he could become an honorary Drug Enforcement Administration (DEA) officer.

In the 1972 reelection campaign, entertainer Sammy Davis Jr., a close Sinatra confidante, embraced Nixon on stage in what became a widely publicized gesture of support from one of Hollywood's signature entertainers.

Dr. Lungren's Refusal to Prescribe Dilantin for Nixon

The British journalist Anthony Summers alleges in his book *The Arrogance of Power: The Secret World of Richard Nixon* (Viking Press, 2000) that Nixon abused the drug Dilantin, an anticonvulsant medication used to prevent epileptic seizures. Summers claims that Nixon took Dilantin without a prescription for depression soon after he was elected President in 1968.

Summers writes that billionaire Jack Dreyfus Jr., founder of the Dreyfus Fund, was the key figure in providing Nixon with Dilantin. Dreyfus, now in his late eighties, has had a deep interest in defining and exploring Dilantin as a "new elixir" with uncounted therapeutic benefits. A true believer, Dreyfus has spent tens of millions of dollars in promoting Dilantin through his own research foundation. Summers alleges that Nixon "consumed large quantities" of the drug "over a long period." Summers supports this hypothesis by citing conversations with Dreyfus, who told him of the alleged 1968 meeting with Nixon during which Dreyfus supposedly informed Nixon of Dilantin's medicinal attributes.

Nixon's medical records reveal no evidence of ingestion or pattern of ingestion of Dilantin. Dilantin may have serious side effects, including slurred speech, diminished coordination, mental confusion, dizziness, insomnia, and nervousness. For Nixon to hide a pattern of such behavior induced by Dilantin would have been impossible, given the scrutiny of a president by his physicians and the media.

The tone of the letter is solicitous in its attempt to persuade Dr. Lungren to prescribe Dilantin for Nixon. The letter's import is that Nixon had never taken Dilantin, but that if Dr. Lungren prescribed Dilantin, he would receive "the remarkable benefits of this substance . . . hidden from the general public."

Dr. Lungren never prescribed Dilantin for Nixon. He had his own regimen of therapy and rehabilitation that addressed both physical and psychological recovery. If everything became clear with his "research," why did Summers not interview Dr. Lungren regarding Dilantin?

Summers surely knew who Dr. Lungren was, because he writes about him as "the president's California physician" in *The Arrogance of Power.*

Notes

Foreword

1. Lawrence K. Altman, "Conflict on Care of Nixon: Town vs. Gown."
2. Herbert S. Parmet, *Nixon and His America.*

Prefaces

1. Tom Wicker, *One of Us: Richard Nixon and the American Dream,* 686.
2. Richard Holmes, *Dr. Johnson and Mr. Savage,* 230–31.
3. Reynolds Price, *A Whole New Life,* 144–45.
4. John Colville, *Winston Churchill and His Inner Circle,* 245.
5. Shakespeare, *Hamlet,* 5.2, 371–72.
6. Richard Nixon, quoting Sophocles in *Six Crises,* 426.

Chapter 1

1. Jonathan Aitken, *Nixon: A Life,* 522.
2. Stephen Ambrose, *Nixon: Ruin and Recovery, 1973–1990,* 193–94.
3. Richard Nixon, *RN: The Memoirs of Richard Nixon,* 1061.

Chapter 2

1. Robert Sam Anson, *Exile,* 31.
2. Ibid., 31–32.
3. Ibid., 19.

4. Henry Kissinger, *Years of Renewal,* 39.
5. Ibid.
6. Leonard Garment, *Crazy Rhythm,* 361.
7. Ecclesiastes 7:17–18, The New Jerusalem Bible.
8. Kissinger, *Years of Renewal,* 39.
9. "Statement by the President in Connection with Nixon Pardon," *New York Times,* 8 September 1974.
10. Nixon, *RN,* 1008.
11. Ibid., 1008.
12. Ibid., 1010.

Chapter 3

1. "That Nixon 'Stone Wall' Rises in L.B.," *The Long Beach Independent Press-Telegram,* 29 September 1974.

Chapter 4

1. John Milton, *Paradise Lost,* book 9, lines 351–59.

Chapter 5

1. Anson, *Exile,* 102.
2. Stephen Ambrose, *Nixon: The Education of a Politician, 1913–1962,* 124.
3. Roger Morris, *Richard Milhous Nixon,* 292.
4. Ralph de Toledano, *One Man Alone: Richard Nixon,* 191.
5. *Newsweek,* "The Nixon Spark."
6. Herbert G. Klein, *Making It Perfectly Clear,* viii, ix.
7. Ibid., xii.
8. Ibid., 83.
9. De Toledano, *One Man Alone,* 209.
10. Ibid.

Chapter 6

1. Mark Bloom, "Should the Health of Presidential Candidates Be a Campaign Issue?" 49.
2. Gore Vidal, "Coached by Camelot," 85.
3. Ibid., 92.
4. Theodore H. White, *The Making of the President, 1960.*

5. Ibid.

6. Don Hewitt, *Tell Me a Story,* 67.

7. Nixon, *RN,* 220.

8. Christopher Matthews, *Kennedy and Nixon,* 163.

9. Nixon, *RN,* 215.

10. William Safire, *Before the Fall,* 563.

11. Ibid.

Chapter 7

1. Anson, *Exile,* 202.

2. Aitken, *Nixon,* 303.

3. Christopher Ogden, *Legacy,* 469.

4. Ibid.

Chapter 8

1. Julie Nixon Eisenhower, *Pat Nixon, the Untold Story,* 434–35.

2. Nixon, *In the Arena,* 23.

Chapter 9

1. Lawrence K. Altman, "Nixon Scheduled to Leave Hospital Today after Doctor Reports Improvement in His Condition."

2. Altman, "Conflict on Care of Nixon: Town vs. Gown."

3. Ibid.

4. Ibid.

5. Richard West and Kathy Burke, "Nixon Leaves Hospital, Will Convalesce at San Clemente."

6. Robert L. Jackson, "Sirica Picks Doctors to Examine Nixon."

7. Altman, "The Check-up on Nixon."

8. Ibid.

9. Raymond Price, *With Nixon,* 32–33.

Chapter 10

1. Letter from Jack Dreyfus to Dr. John C. Lungren, 6 January 1975.

Chapter 11

1. 8-0 ruling, *United States v. Richard Nixon* (1974).
2. *New York Times Co. v. United States* (1971).
3. Gabor S. Boritt, *Lincoln: The War President,* 158–59.
4. Ibid.

Chapter 12

1. Max Frankel, *The Times of My Life and My Life with* The Times, 349–50.
2. Garment, *Crazy Rhythm,* 197.

Chapter 13

1. Nixon, *In the Arena,* 25.
2. Henry Kissinger, *The World Restored,* 213.
3. Maurice Blanchot, *The Writing of the Disaster,* 13.
4. Nixon, *RN,* 1054–1055.

Chapter 14

1. Nixon, *Six Crises,* xvi.
2. Nixon, *In the Arena,* 139.
3. Nixon, *Six Crises,* xx.
4. Nixon, *In the Arena,* 31.
5. Dan was elected attorney general of California in 1990 and was reelected in 1994. He ran for governor of California in 1998 but lost to Gray Davis.

Chapter 15

1. Brian later became a police officer with the Los Angeles Police Department and earned a master's degree in public administration from Pepperdine University.
2. Shakespeare, *King Lear,* 4.6.83–89.
3. Ibid., 3.2.57–60.
4. Ibid., 4.2.3–6.

Chapter 16

1. Dr. Li Zhisui, *Private Life of Chairman Mao,* 564.

2. Stephen E. Ambrose, *Nixon: Ruin and Recovery, 1973–1990,* 492.
   3. James M. Naughton. "Nixon Trip Revives Issue Vexing to Ford in Primary."
   4. Alex Ross, "Nixon Is Everywhere, It Seems, but in 'China.'"

Chapter 17

1. Statement made by Billy Graham at the funeral of Patricia Ryan Nixon, 26 June 1993. http://www.nixonfoundation.org/Research_Center/Nixons/PatNixonFuneral.shtml
   2. Diedre Carmody, review of *The Final Days,* by Woodward and Bernstein.
   3. David Halberstam, interviewed by Brian Lamb on the C-Span program *Booknotes,* 11 July 1993.
   4. Ibid.

Chapter 18

1. Whittaker Chambers, *Cold Friday,* 68.
   2. Sophocles, *Oedipus Rex,* Exodus, 63.
   3. Shakespeare, *King Lear,* 4.5.80.
   4. Blanchot, *The Writing of the Disaster,* 14.
   5. Sir Charles Wilson. *Churchill,* 732.
   6. Ibid., xi–xii.
   7. Nixon, *Beyond Peace,* 153.
   8. Sir Charles Wilson, *Churchill,* 177–78.
   9. Nixon, *Beyond Peace,* 153.
   10. John Paul II, *Ut Unum Sint,* 13.
   11. Nixon, *Beyond Peace,* 155–56.
   12. James Chace and Nicholas X. Rizopoulos, "Toward a New Concert of Nations," 8.
   13. Nixon. *Beyond Peace,* 169.
   14. Paul Sherman. *The Shores of America,* 416–17.
   15. Jean-Paul Kaufmann, *The Black Room at Longwood.*
   16. R.W. Apple Jr., "Richard Nixon, 81, Dies."
   17. Shakespeare, *King Lear,* 5.3.314.
   18. "Eulogies Taken from Memorial Services in the Congress of the United States and Tributes in Eulogy of Richard M. Nixon: Late a President of the United States," United States Government Printing Office.

19. Ibid.

20. Ibid.

21. Ibid.

22. Maureen Dowd, "Rainy Prologue to Subdued Funeral for Nixon."

23. Denise Levertov, "Making Peace," line 425.

24. Ibid., lines 22–29.

25. Eugenio Montale, "The Lemon Tree," *Cuttlefish Bones*, 9.

26. "Transcript of Nixon's Farewell Speech to Cabinet and Staff Members in the Capital," *New York Times,* 9 August 74.

27. Zbigniew Herbert, *Selected Poems,* 24.

Bibliography

Books

Abrahamsen, David. *Nixon vs. Nixon: An Emotional Tragedy.* New York: Farrar, Straus, and Giroux, 1977.

Adams, John. *Nixon in China: An Opera in Three Acts.* New York: Warner Communications, 1987.

Aitken, Jonathan. *Nixon: A Life.* Washington, D.C.: Regnery Publishing, 1993.

Ambrose, Stephen E. *Nixon: The Education of a Politician, 1913–1962.* New York: Simon & Schuster, 1987.

———. *Nixon: Ruin and Recovery, 1973–1990.* New York: Simon and Schuster, 1991.

Anson, Robert Sam. *Exile: The Unquiet Oblivion of Richard M. Nixon.* New York: Simon and Schuster, 1984.

Blanchot, Maurice. *The Writing of the Disaster.* Translated by Ann Smock. Lincoln: University of Nebraska Press, 1995.

Boritt, Gabor S. *Lincoln: The War President.* New York: Oxford University Press, 1992.

Chambers, Whittaker. *Cold Friday.* New York: Random House, 1964.

Colville, John. *Winston Churchill and His Inner Circle.* New York: Wyndham Books, 1981.

Coover, Robert. *The Public Burning.* New York: Grove Press, 1977.

De Toledano, Ralph. *One Man Alone: Richard Nixon.* New York: Funk and Wagnall, 1969.

Dylan, Bob. *Writings and Drawings.* New York: Alfred Knopf, Inc., 1973.

Eisenhower, Julie Nixon. *Pat Nixon: The Untold Story.* New York: Simon and Schuster, 1986.

Fitzwater, Marlin. *Call the Briefing! Reagan and Bush, Sam and Helen: A Decade with Presidents and the Press.* Holbrook, Mass.: Adams Media Corporation, 1995.

Frankel, Max. *The Times of My Life and My Life with The Times.* New York: Random House, 1997.

Garment, Leonard. *Crazy Rhythm: My Journey from Brooklyn, Jazz, and Wall Street to Nixon's White House.* New York: Times Books, Division of Random House, 1997.

Haldeman, H.R. *The Haldeman Diaries: Inside the Nixon White House.* New York: G.P. Putnam's Sons, 1994.

Herbert, Zbigniew. *Selected Poems.* Translated by Czeslaw Milosz and Peter Dale Scott. Hopewell, N.J.: The Ecco Press, 1968.

Hewitt, Don. *Tell Me a Story.* New York: Public Affairs, a member of the Perseus Books Group, 2001.

Holmes, Richard. *Dr. Johnson and Mr. Savage.* New York: Vintage Books, 1996.

John Paul II. *Encyclical Letter: Ut Unum Sint.* Boston: Pauline Books, 1995.

Kauffmann, Jean-Paul. *The Black Room at Longwood: Napolean's Exile on Saint Helena.* Translated by Patricia Clancy. New York: Four Walls Eight Windows, 1999.

Kissinger, Henry. *The World Restored: Metternich, Castlereagh, and the Problems of Peace, 1812–22.* Boston: Houghton Mifflin Co, 1973.

———. *Years of Renewal.* New York: Simon & Schuster, 1999.

Klein, Herbert G. *Making It Perfectly Clear.* New York: Doubleday & Company, 1980.

Levertov, Denise. "Making Peace." *The Heath Anthology of American Literature,* vol. 2, ed. Paul Lauter. Lexington, Mass.: D.C. Heath and Co., 1994.

Matthews, Christopher. *Kennedy and Nixon: The Rivalry That*

Shaped Postwar America. New York: Simon and Schuster, 1996.

Montale, Eugenio. *Cuttlefish Bones.* Translated by William Arrowsmith. New York: W.W. Norton and Co., 1992.

Morris, Roger. *Richard Milhous Nixon: The Rise of an American Politician.* New York: Henry Holt and Co., 1990.

Nixon, Richard. *Beyond Peace.* New York: Random House, 1994.

————. *In the Arena: A Memoir of Victory, Defeat, and Renewal.* New York: Simon and Schuster, 1990.

————. *RN: The Memoirs of Richard Nixon.* New York: Grosset and Dunlap, 1978.

————. *Six Crises.* New York: Simon & Schuster, 1990.

Ogden, Christopher. *Legacy: A Biography of Moses and Walter Annenberg.* New York: Little Brown & Co., 1999.

Parmet, Herbert. *Richard Nixon and His America.* Boston: Little, Brown, and Co., 1990.

Price, Raymond. *With Nixon.* New York: The Viking Press, 1977.

Price, Reynolds. *A Whole New Life.* New York: Scribner, 1994.

Rehnquist, William H. *All the Laws But One: Civil Liberties in Wartime.* New York: Alfred A. Knopf, 1998.

Safire, William. *Before the Fall: An Inside View of the Pre-Watergate White House.* New York: Doubleday and Co., 1975.

Sherman, Paul. *The Shores of America: Thoreau's Inward Exploration.* New York: Russell and Russell, 1971.

Wannall, Ray. *The Real J. Edgar Hoover for the Record.* Paducah, Ky.: Turner Publishing, 2000.

White, Theodore H. *The Making of the President, 1960.* New York: Atheneum, 1961.

————. *The Making of the President, 1968.* New York: Atheneum, 1969.

Wilson, Sir Charles (Lord Moran). *Churchill: Taken from the Diaries of Lord Moran.* Dunwoody, Ga.: Norman S. Berg, Publisher, 1976.

Witcover, Jules. *The Resurrection of Richard Nixon.* New York: G.P. Putnam's Sons, 1970.

Zhisui, Dr. Li. *The Private Life of Chairman Mao.* Translated by Tai Hung-chao. New York: Random House, 1994.

Periodicals

Altman, Lawrence K. "Conflict on Care of Nixon: Town vs. Gown." *New York Times,* 16 November 1974.
————. "Nixon Scheduled to Leave Hospital Today After Doctor Reports Improvement in His Condition." *New York Times,* 14 November 1974.
————. "The Check-up on Nixon." *New York Times,* 30 November 1974
Apple, R.W. Jr. "Richard Nixon, 81, Dies: A Master of Politics Undone by Watergate." *New York Times,* 23 April 1994.
Bloom, Mark. "Should the Health of Presidential Candidates Be a Campaign Issue?" *Medical World News,* 9 February 1976, 34–54.
Carmody, Diedre. Review of *The Final Days,* by Bob Woodward and Carl Bernstein. *New York Times,* April 1976.
Chace, James and Nicholas X. Rizopoulos. "Toward a New Concert of Nations," *World Policy Journal* 16, no. 3 (fall 1999): 2–10.
Dowd, Maureen. "Rainy Prologue to Subdued Funeral for Nixon." *New York Times,* 26 April 1994.
Jackson, Robert L. "Sirica Picks Doctors to Examine Nixon." *Los Angeles Times,* 14 November 1974, Part 1, 14.
Naughton, James M. "Nixon Trip Revives Issue Vexing to Ford in Primary." *New York Times,* 21 February 1976.
"Nixon Medical Files Rifled Here in 1972." *Long Beach Independent Press-Telegram,* 4 May 1973.
"The Nixon Spark." *Newsweek.* 15 November 1954.
Ross, Alex. "Nixon Is Everywhere, It Seems, but in 'China.'" *New York Times,* 7 April 1996.
"Statement by the President in Connection with Nixon Pardon." *New York Times,* 8 September 1974.

"That Nixon 'Stone Wall' Rises in L.B." *Long Beach Independent Press Telegram,* 29 September 1974.

"Transcript of Nixon's Farewell Speech to Cabinet and Staff Members in the Capital." *New York Times,* 9 August 1974.

Vidal, Gore. "Coached by Camelot," a review of *The Dark Side of Camelot* by Seymour M. Hersh. *The New Yorker,* 1 December 1997, 84–92.

West, Richard and Kathy Burke. "Nixon Leaves Hospital. Will Convalesce at San Clemente." *Los Angeles Times,* 14 November 1974.

Index